1. The four most important typographic choices you make in any document are POINT SIZE (90), LINE SPACING (139), LINE LENGTH (141), and font (passim), because those choices determine how the BODY TEXT (145) looks.

2. POINT SIZE (90) should be between 10 and 12 points in printed documents.

3. LINE SPACING (139) should be 120–145% of the point size.

4. The average LINE LENGTH (141) should be 45–90 characters (including spaces).

5. On 8.5″×11″ paper, PAGE MARGINS (142) should be larger than one inch.

6. Avoid GOOFY FONTS (79) and MONO-SPACED FONTS (80).

7. Avoid SYSTEM FONTS (82) if you can.

8. Use curly quotation marks, not straight ones (38).

9. Put only ONE SPACE BETWEEN SENTENCES (41).

10. Don't use multiple WORD SPACES (63) or other WHITE-SPACE CHARACTERS (61) in a row.

11. Never UNDERLINE (78).

12. Use CENTERED TEXT (134) sparingly.

13. Use BOLD OR ITALIC (85) as little as possible.

14. ALL CAPS (86) are fine for less than one line of text.

15. If you don't have real SMALL CAPS (104), don't use them at all.

16. Use 5 with .... (...) ... . (104).

17. Use FIRST-LINE INDENTS (136) that are one to four times the POINT SIZE (90) of the text, or use between four and ten points of SPACE BETWEEN PARA-GRAPHS (138)—but don't use both.

18. If you use JUSTIFIED TEXT (135), also turn on HYPHENATION (146).

19. Don't confuse HYPHENS AND DASHES (48).

20. Use AMPERSANDS (52) sparingly, unless included in a proper name or a citation format.

21. In a document longer than three pages, one exclamation point is plenty (44).

22. Use proper TRADEMARK AND COPY-RIGHT SYMBOLS (50)—not alphabetic substitutes.

23. Put a NONBREAKING SPACE (63) after PARAGRAPH AND SECTION MARKS (46).

24. Make ELLIPSES (53) using the proper character, not periods and spaces.

25. Use a sequence of underscores to make a SIGNATURE LINE (55).

26. Make sure APOSTROPHES (56) point downward.

27. Make sure FOOT AND INCH MARKS (60) are straight, not curly.

28. KERNING (97) should always be turned on.

To Jessica—
my best friend & my favorite lawyer.

Contents

Foreword by Bryan A. Garner

IF MATTHEW BUTTERICK DIDN'T EXIST, IT WOULD BE necessary to invent him. What's unusual about the tour de force you're now holding is that not only is it bold and fresh and original, but also it's fully developed: it reads like a fifth edition. It's smartly reasoned, it's backed up by years of cultivated expertise, and it's well written.

Here's how to use this book if you're a supervising lawyer (Sarah) dealing with an associate (Ralph):

"Ralph, thanks for the memo. I'm looking forward to reading it. But ..."

"Is there a problem?"

"Well yes. Frankly, I don't want to read it. You're underlining case names, you're putting two spaces after periods, and the font is just ghastly. I could spend 30 minutes making it presentable, but I want the associates who work with me to do that in the first place. Do you own Butterick?"

"Huh?"

"Butterick. *Typography for Lawyers*. Here, take my copy home tonight. I'll need it back tomorrow. Learn this stuff, please. I want all your writing for me to comply with Butterick. Got that?"

"Sure, Sarah. Thanks. I'll see you tomorrow."

Tomorrow will be a very new day.

Here's how to proceed if you're an associate (Leslie) dealing with a supervisor (Russell):

"Leslie, I don't like the formatting of this memo. I want double-spaced Courier. And two spaces after a period!"

[Smiling pleasantly.] "You're kidding!"

"No, that's the way I want documents formatted."

[Smiling pleasantly but incredulously.] "Is that just for editing purposes? I mean, we're about to send this off to the client!"

"That's the final format for transmitting it to the client." [He would say *transmitting*, wouldn't he?]

"Russ, bear with me. You're the partner here, but haven't you read Butterick? I really think we should follow Butterick. It makes the firm look better."

"Who the hell is Butterick?"

"You know, *Typography for Lawyers*. He's the guy who sets the standards for document design in law offices. He makes a good case that most lawyers are completely in the dark about typography. Here, have a look at it."

Russell demurs.

"Really, Russ, I was shocked to learn that there should be only one space after a period. He makes an irrefutable case. Here, read just page 41." [Be sure to say /ir-**ref**-yə-tə-bəl/, for credibility's sake.]

[Russell reads.] "I don't care. I want double-spaced Courier. And two spaces after a period."

"OK, Russ." [Beaming enthusiastically.] "But I'm telling you, you've got to read Butterick."

Here's how to proceed if you're on a committee that will be producing a report. At the tail end of the first meeting, as people are packing up, you say: "Can we make everyone's life easier with just one ground rule? We will follow Butterick in all our drafts and in the final report. OK?"

"Butterick?"

"Sure. *Typography for Lawyers*. It'll make our committee work so much more pleasant when we're exchanging drafts. You don't know Butterick? I'll get you a copy. Believe me: it'll change your life. You'll wonder how you ever did without it."

"You're kidding."

"Absolutely not. You'd do well to learn Butterick!"

Please remember these bits of dialogue. Adapt them. Use them. Often.

Is Butterick infallible? No: on page 106 he recommends three-level decimals. But otherwise he's assuredly infallible.

— BRYAN A. GARNER

Introduction

AS LAWYERS, WE KNOW THAT WRITING IS CENTRAL TO OUR work. Whether it's a sixty-page brief for the United States Supreme Court, or a two-line confirmation of a client meeting tapped out in an airport terminal, our jobs require a steady flow of clear, professional written communications.

But we do more than write. We edit, we rewrite, we format, we print, we copy, we fax, we mail, we file. We take responsibility for all the steps between us and our readers (and we're liable for the consequences if we don't). That means we're more than just writers—we're publishers.

In fact, we're part of the biggest, most important publishing industry in the United States. According to the Bureau of Labor Statistics, in May 2009, the print-publishing industry (including books, newspapers, and magazines) employed 801,600 people at an average hourly wage of $32.08. Meanwhile, 999,020 people were employed in law-related jobs at an average hourly wage of $46.07, including 556,790 lawyers.

Even those figures don't fully express how much is riding on our work. Some of us handle issues that involve life and death, or civil rights and oppression, or jobs and livelihoods. But regardless of the stakes, all of us are handling issues that are important to someone—our clients.

In short, our work matters.
Because our work matters, our writing matters.
Because our writing matters, our typography matters.

I'm not here to tell you that typography is at the core of a lawyer's work. It's not. But typography can optimize that work. All writing necessarily involves typography. And good writing is part of good lawyering. So good typography is too. If you ignore typography, you are ignoring an opportunity to improve both your writing and your advocacy.

This book is based on three core principles.

①   Good typography is part of good lawyering.

②   Typography in legal documents should be held to the same standards as any professionally published material. Why? Because legal documents *are* professionally published material.

    (Corollary: much of what lawyers consider proper legal typography is an accumulation of bad habits and urban legends. These will be set aside in favor of professional typographic habits.)

③   Any lawyer can master the essentials of good typography.

The first chapter of this book, WHY TYPOGRAPHY MATTERS, explains what typography is and why you should care.

The next three chapters cover typographic rules. TYPE COMPOSITION covers the symbols and characters available on the keyboard. TEXT FORMATTING covers the appearance of characters and text, and includes a gallery of recommended fonts. PAGE LAYOUT covers the broader issues that surface when putting documents together. In each chapter, rather than grouping the rules into topics and subtopics, I've sequenced them roughly in order of difficulty, and grouped them into basic and advanced sets.

The last chapter, SAMPLE DOCUMENTS, brings everything together by working through before-and-after examples of common legal documents.

Small caps (e.g., WHY TYPOGRAPHY MATTERS) signal a cross-reference to another section. The inside back cover has an alphabetical index of cross-references.

There's more than one right way to use this book. Some will want to learn everything in TYPE COMPOSITION before moving on to TEXT FORMATTING. Others will want to master the basic rules in each chapter before trying the advanced rules. Others will want to open the book only when a specific typographic issue arises.

Regardless of the path you take, the easiest way to learn typography is to practice. Don't just read the rules. Find typographic problems and solve them.

The typographic rules in this book are not specific to particular software. You can apply these rules in just about any modern page-layout program or word processor.

I've included specific technical tips for five popular word processors: Microsoft Word 2003, 2007, and 2010 (all for Windows); Corel WordPerfect X5 (for Windows); and Apple Pages '09 (for the Mac). Tips for Word apply to all versions unless specified.

I have not included tips for Microsoft Word on the Mac.

But the focus of this book is typography. It's not intended as a replacement for your software manual or help file. I've skipped technical issues that are especially basic (such as how to apply BOLD OR ITALIC formatting) or especially complicated (such as how to implement PARAGRAPH AND CHARACTER STYLES).

In FONT SAMPLES and SAMPLE DOCUMENTS, certain visual examples are accompanied by a code number. These codes will take you to further information and PDF samples on the Typography for Lawyers website. To use a code, go to:

`http://typographyforlawyers.com/code/`

Enter the code number in the box that appears.

Legal documents lie along a continuum from more typographically flexible (e.g., LETTERHEAD, RESEARCH MEMOS) to less flexible (e.g., MOTIONS). Not every recommendation in this book will suit every document. Use your judgment.

I sometimes illustrate typographic ideas with examples from California litigation because I'm familiar with it. But my recommendations are meant to be adaptable to any type of practice in any jurisdiction.

That said, this book is not legal advice. If what I suggest conflicts with laws or court rules in your jurisdiction, ignore me and obey the law—obviously.

What qualifies me to write about typography? I have a visual-arts degree from Harvard, where I learned traditional letterpress printing and digital font design. My typographic work is in the permanent collection of the Houghton Library at Harvard. After college, I worked as a font designer for several years in Boston. I then opened a website-development studio in San Francisco. That studio eventually became part of a larger technology company. A few years later, I started law school at UCLA. I'm now an attorney in Los Angeles. Along the way, I've written frequently about text, typography, and related topics.

The golden thread connecting these activities is my affection for the written word. Technology evolves, but text remains irreplaceable.

This book is based on the Typography for Lawyers website, which I started in fall 2008. At the time, I thought it would appeal to a handful of curious lawyers. But the response has been both overwhelming and overwhelmingly positive. I've heard from lawyers (and nonlawyers) all over the world about how this information is making a difference in their work. The website has been recommended in books, in magazines, on blogs, and elsewhere. I'm tremendously grateful to everyone who has spread the word. This book would not exist without your enthusiasm.

Typography has been a source of enjoyment for me for over 20 years. I hope that you also find it rewarding, and that it adds satisfaction—and maybe even some fun—to your practice.

— MATTHEW BUTTERICK
LOS ANGELES, OCTOBER 2010

17

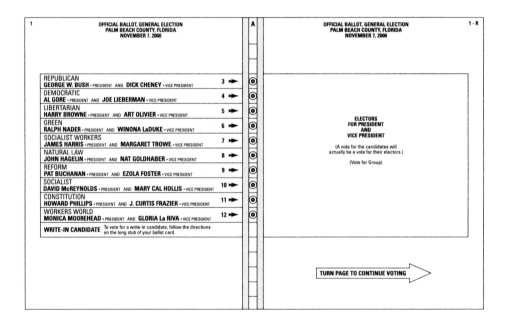

TOP   A recreation of the "butterfly ballot" from Palm Beach County, Florida.

BOTTOM   A butterfly-free redesign by William Lidwell, Kritina Holden, and Jill Butler, featured in their book *Universal Principles of Design* (see BIBLIOGRAPHY).

Why typography matters

YOU ARE ALREADY A TYPOGRAPHER. You may be a reluctant typographer. You may be an unskilled typographer. But every time you put words on a printed page, you've made typography happen. So you are a typographer.

This book is about making you a better typographer. And if you're wondering "what's in it for me?", this chapter will tell you.

Typography is not just the icing on the cake that is your text. Typography has consequences. Just ask the person who was responsible for the ballot used in Palm Beach County, Florida, for the 2000 presidential election.

The typography of the infamous "butterfly ballot" wasn't random. Like every terrible and misguided project throughout history, it seemed like a good idea at the time. Someone considered a number of typographic alternatives and approved this one.

Typography helps you engage readers, guide them, and ultimately persuade them. The more you appreciate what typography can do, the better a typographer you can become.

And you can ensure that you never turn your own work into the equivalent of a butterfly ballot.

what is typography?

The visual component of written texts

Typography is the visual component of the written word.

A text is a sequence of words. A text stays the same no matter how it's rendered. Consider the sentence "I like pizza." I can print that text on a piece of paper, or read it aloud, or save it in a file on my laptop. It'll be the same text, just rendered different ways—visually, audibly, digitally.

But when "I like pizza" is printed, typography gets involved. All visually displayed text involves typography—whether it's on paper, a computer screen, or a billboard.

For example, what's the difference between these two signs: the text or the typography?

Is typography an art? That's like asking if photography is an art. Certainly there are photographers and typographers whose ideas and techniques raise their work to the level of art. But at their core, both photography and typography perform a utilitarian function. The aesthetic component is separate. Being an effective typographer is more about good skills than good taste.

BY THE WAY

➡ Don't infer from the highway-sign example that *typography* is another word for *font*. Fonts are part of typography, but typography goes beyond fonts.

Typography is *for the benefit of the reader*, not the writer.

This is an obvious principle if you're a professional typographer who didn't write the text. Then you can approach it as a special kind of reader—one whose job it is to design the visual component of the text so it reinforces the meaning.

It's a more difficult principle if you're a writer who has to handle your own typography. Then you have to negotiate the conflict between your primary perspective as a writer and a simulated perspective as a reader.

"But every writer is also a reader—I end up reading the text several times while I'm rewriting it." In a mechanical sense, yes, you're reading the text. But you're reading it only so you can rewrite it. You're not reading it for the same reasons as your reader—to learn and possibly to be persuaded.

who is typography for?

*Readers,
not writers*

In fact, your reader is quite different from you:

	WRITER	READER
Attention span	Long	Short
Interest in topic	High	Low
Persuadable by other opinions	No	Yes
Cares about making your client happy	Yes	No

Unfortunately, legal writers sometimes imagine that the comparison looks like this:

	WRITER	READER
Attention span	Long	Whatever it takes
Interest in topic	High	Boundless
Persuadable by other opinions	No	Barely
Cares about making your client happy	Yes	Of course

The only reader who might match that description is your mother.

Typography has to be oriented to your actual readers, not idealized ones. Writers often get attached to idealized readers because those readers are easier to please. Don't be lazy. Work hard to see your text as an actual reader will. You won't get it perfectly right. But a rough approximation is better than no approximation at all.

Typography matters because it helps conserve the most valuable resource you have as a writer—*reader attention.*

Attention is the reader's gift to you. That gift is precious. It is finite. And should you fail to be an adequate steward of that gift, it will be promptly revoked.

Once a reader revokes the gift of attention, you don't have a reader anymore. You remain a writer only in the narrowest sense of the word. Yes, you scattered some words across some pages. But if the reader has disappeared, then what was the point? How is your "writing" more valuable than a random string of characters? No one's there to notice the difference.

Many legal writers adopt a riskier model of reader attention. Instead of treating reader attention as precious, they treat it as an unlimited resource. "I'll take as much attention as I need, and if I want more, I'll take that too."

What could be more presumptuous? Or dangerous?

Writing as if you have unlimited reader attention is presumptuous because readers are not doing you a personal favor. Reading your writing is not their hobby. It's their job. And their job involves paying attention to lots of other writing. The judge has not set aside your motion for summary judgment so she can savor it during her upcoming vacation to Maui. More likely, it is just one item in a queue of hundreds, all of which require her attention.

I'll even go one better: I believe that most readers are *looking for reasons to stop reading.* Not because they're malicious or aloof. They're just being rational. If readers have other demands on their time, why should they pay any more attention than they absolutely must? Readers are always looking for the exit.

Conserves reader attention

Writing as if you have unlimited reader attention is also dangerous, because running out of reader attention is fatal to your writing. The goal of legal writing is persuasion, and attention is a prerequisite for persuasion. Once the reader's attention expires, you have no chance to persuade. You're just giving a monologue in an empty theater.

If you believe reader attention is a valuable resource, then tools that help you conserve that resource are likewise valuable. Typography is one of those tools.

Good typography can help your reader devote less attention to the mechanics of reading and more attention to your message. Conversely, bad typography can distract your reader and undermine your message.

I'm not suggesting that the quality of your typography is more important than the quality of your writing. It's not. But typography can make good writing even better.

Consider an oral argument in court. By the day of the hearing, you'll have spent a lot of time honing the structure and substance of your argument. But do you show up to court in jeans and sneakers? No, of course not. You wear proper court attire. And when you speak to the judge, do you slouch at the lectern, eyes cast downward, and read from a script in a monotone? No, of course not. You change the speed and volume of your delivery. You gesture. You extemporize.

You do these things because you don't merely want to be heard— you want to persuade. To persuade, you need to hold the judge's attention. And to hold that attention, you cannot undermine your argument with distractions.

It's the same on the printed page. The text matters, but if that's all that mattered, then everything could be set in 12-point TIMES NEW ROMAN. And that would be the equivalent of staring at the lectern.

In the same way that good speaking skills matter during an oral argument, good typography matters in a written document.

"But I don't have visual skills. I don't know anything about graphic design." That's like saying you can't dress properly for court because you don't know anything about fashion design.

Compared to studying for the bar exam, it's easy to learn the skills necessary for producing good typography. Beyond those skills, you need only the ability to form opinions about typography. And everyone who reads—even kids—can do this.

Unconvinced? Try this. On the next two pages are two résumés that you've received for an associate opening at your firm. Being a busy person, you only have two seconds to decide who gets the last interview slot. Who do you pick? Don't read the résumés—you don't have time. Just make a two-second decision.

VIOLET S. MANGANESE

5419 HOLLYWOOD BLVD. STE. C731, LOS ANGELES CA 90027   (323) 555-1435   VIOLET @GMAIL.COM

Education

UCLA School of Law   Los Angeles, California
August 2007 to June 2010
- ❖ Cumulative GPA: 3.98
- ❖ Academic interests: real-estate financing, criminal procedure, corporations
- ❖ California Bar Exam results pending

Harvard University   Cambridge, Massachusetts
September 2002 to June 2006
- ❖ B.A. summa cum laude, Economics
- ❖ Extensive coursework in Astrophysics, Statistics
- ❖ Van Damme Scholarship

Legal experience

Falkenburg, Fester & Funk LLP   New York, New York
November 2008 to present
Law clerk
- ❖ Handled various litigation matters in state and federal court, including:
- ❖ An unlawful detainer action
- ❖ A demurrer to a breach-of-contract lawsuit in state court
- ❖ Oppositions to motions to dismiss in federal court (Fed. R. Civ. P. 12(b), 12(e), 9(b))
- ❖ Development of evidence for Internet trademark and copyright infringement actions, including statistical analysis

Other work experience

Proximate Cause   Los Angeles, California
June 2006 to May 2007
Assistant to the Director
- ❖ Helped devise fundraising campaigns for this innovative nonprofit
- ❖ Handled lunch orders and general errands

Hot Topic   Boston, Massachusetts
February 2003 to March 2005
Retail sales associate
- ❖ Top in-store sales associate in seven out of eight quarters
- ❖ Inventory management
- ❖ Training and recruiting

Skills and interests

- ❖ Fluent in Mandarin, Esperanto; conversational knowledge of Gaelic
- ❖ Writer of U.S. Senate-themed fan fiction
- ❖ Ocean kayaking and free diving
- ❖ Travel, cooking, hiking, playing with my dog
- ❖ Ceramics

TRIXIE B. ARGON

5419 HOLLYWOOD BLVD. STE. C731, LOS ANGELES CA 90027

(323) 555-1435   TRIXIEARGON @ GMAIL.COM

Education

UCLA School of Law   2007–10

- Cumulative GPA: 3.98
- Academic interests: real-estate financing, criminal procedure, corporations
- California Bar Exam results pending

Harvard University   2002–06

- B.A. *summa cum laude*, Economics
- Extensive coursework in Astrophysics, Statistics
- Van Damme Scholarship

Legal experience

Falkenburg, Fester & Funk LLP   2008–now

Law clerk

- Handled various litigation matters in state and federal court, including:
- An unlawful detainer action
- A demurrer to a breach-of-contract lawsuit in state court
- Oppositions to motions to dismiss in federal court (Fed. R. Civ. P. 12(b), 12(e), 9(b))
- Development of evidence for Internet trademark and copyright infringement actions, including statistical analysis

Other work experience

Proximate Cause   2006–07

Assistant to the Director

- Helped devise fundraising campaigns for this innovative nonprofit
- Handled lunch orders and general errands

Hot Topic   2003–05

Retail sales associate

- Top in-store sales associate in seven out of eight quarters
- Inventory management
- Training and recruiting

Whose résumé got your attention—Violet's (on the left) or Trixie's (on the right)? Whose résumé better persuaded you, in two seconds, that the candidate was worth interviewing?

I'm guessing you picked Trixie's. But why? Maybe you'd say Trixie's résumé looked more professional, neater, or better organized. All true, but those qualities don't appear out of thin air. And if you look again, you'll see that the credentials on the résumés are identical. The only difference is the typography.

So what happened? The résumé with the better typography attracted the better quality of attention. Trixie will be getting that interview; Violet will not. Not only did you just prove that typography matters, you proved that it matters *to you*.

And if typography matters to you as a reader—a literate adult with no special visual skills or training—it matters to every other similarly situated reader. Including everyone who reads your work.

Writers skeptical of typography often say, "No one cares how a text looks, they just focus on the substance." This is plainly absurd. Our experiences as readers repeatedly prove the opposite is true. The Violet–Trixie test is just one example.

Typography matters. The only question is whether you, as a writer—and as a lawyer—are going to neglect it.

Good typography *reinforces the goals of the text*.

Almost all texts communicate a set of points (*Summary judgment should be denied for three reasons*). Sometimes a text also needs to instruct the reader (*Add lines 7 through 21 and enter the total here*). Other texts offer warnings or admonitions (*You must be 48 inches tall to ride*; *Speed limit 75*). In every case, good typography supports and reinforces the message. Good typography makes the text more effective.

Three subsidiary propositions flow from this:

① Good typography is measured by how well it reinforces the goals of the text, not by some abstract scale of merit. Typographic choices that work for one text won't necessarily work for another. Corollary: good typographers don't rely on rote solutions. One size never fits all.

② For a given text, there are many typographic solutions that would be equally good. Typography is not a math problem with one correct answer.

③ Your ability to produce good typography depends on how well you understand the goals of your text, not on taste or visual training. Corollary: if you misunderstand the goals of your text, good typography becomes purely a matter of luck.

Pause to absorb the ramifications of proposition #3. Typography is visual, so it's easy to conclude that it's primarily an artistic or aesthetic pursuit. Not so. Typography is primarily utilitarian.

Therefore, good typography is measured on a utilitarian yardstick. Typography that is aesthetically pleasant, but that doesn't reinforce the goals of the text, is a failure. Typography that reinforces the goals of the text, even if aesthetically unpleasant, is a success.

Does that mean that effective typography can be ugly? Sure. Sometimes ugly is better than pretty.

Look at the highway signs again.

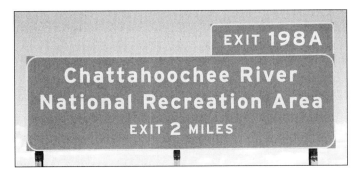

The script font used on the second sign could be called "prettier" than the standard highway-signage font. But a highway sign has a special purpose: it's meant to be read quickly, from long distances, at odd angles, and under variable lighting and weather conditions. The highway-signage font stays legible under all these conditions. It constitutes good typography because it supports the goals of the sign.

The script font may be prettier, but in this context, it's bad typography, because it's not suited to the task. Conversely, the highway-signage font would look terrible on a wedding invitation, where the script font would be appropriate.

A related example:

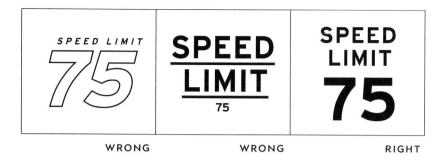

WRONG   WRONG   RIGHT

Here, the same font is used in all three versions of this sign. But the first two signs fail to deliver the message—*the speed limit is 75*—because the typography undermines the text. The most important element is the number *75*. Also important is the caption *speed limit*. Only the third version gets the balance right. It's the only example of good typography among the three.

Use this principle to test the quality of your own typographic work. The advantage of applying a utilitarian benchmark instead of an aesthetic one is that it doesn't require aesthetic judgment. Believe me, if you're just starting out in typography, you will produce some ugly work. Don't worry. If it's ugly *and* effective, you're making progress.

Ask yourself: what are readers looking to get out of your document? All readers want something—that's their incentive to start reading in the first place. Are you giving your readers what they want?

Suppose you're filing a motion in court. What are the goals of the text with respect to the judge?

① Tell the judge what relief you're seeking.

② Persuade the judge that you're entitled to the relief.

"[P]rinting … is important, first and foremost, as a means of doing something. … [I]t is mischievous to call any printed piece a work of art, especially fine art: because that would imply that its first purpose was to exist as an expression of beauty for its own sake."

—Beatrice Warde, "The Crystal Goblet"

That's really it, isn't it? We could break those into component goals, but at the top level, it's simple. And if those are your goals, which of the following typographic options is better?

OPTION 1

YOU ARE HEREBY NOTIFIED that at a date and time to be determined, in Dept. 21 of the above-entitled court, plaintiff **TRIXIE ARGON** will move the Court for an order that defendant **MEGACORP** produce financial records requested by Ms. Argon and reimburse Ms. Argon's costs to bring this motion. This motion is made on the ground that Ms. Argon served MegaCorp with a valid notice to produce financial records at trial. Cal. Civ. Proc. Code § 1987(c); Cal. Civ. Code § 3295(c). MegaCorp served objections and refused to comply.

OPTION 2

You are hereby notified that at a date and time to be determined, in Dept. 21 of the above-entitled court, plaintiff Trixie Argon will move the Court for an order that defendant MegaCorp:

1. **Produce financial records** requested by Ms. Argon and

2. **Reimburse Ms. Argon's costs** to bring this motion.

This motion is made on the ground that Ms. Argon served MegaCorp with a valid notice to produce financial records at trial. Cal. Civ. Proc. Code § 1987(c); Cal. Civ. Code § 3295(c). MegaCorp served objections and refused to comply.

The sample paragraph above could also be edited to improve how it reads. This example is just meant to show what typography alone can accomplish.

Option 1 emphasizes the first four words—who cares about those?—and the party names, which would've been emphasized adequately on the CAPTION PAGE. Given our two stated goals, the typography in Option 1 neither helps the judge understand what relief we're seeking, nor helps persuade the judge we're entitled to the relief. Therefore, this typography fails.

Option 2, however, removes the unnecessary emphasis from the first part of the paragraph, and uses white space, a numbered list,

32   WHY TYPOGRAPHY MATTERS

and bold styling to draw the judge's attention to the relief we're seeking. Therefore, this typography is better, because it reinforces one of the goals of the text.

➡ Reinforcing the goals of the text is a simple principle, but typography in legal documents often undermines the text. For instance, lawyers drafting agreements will often put important paragraphs in ALL CAPS. But all-caps text is more tiring to read than regular text. (Don't take my word for it—flip to page 87 and see for yourself.) So the most likely result of this typographic choice is that readers will pay *less* attention to the important paragraphs in the agreement, not more.

What people know about typography can usually be traced back to typing-class teachers (or computer-lab teachers) and other unreliable sources. I'm sure your teachers were lovely people, but they were there to teach you typing (or BASIC programming), not typography. And what they knew about typography probably came from their own typing teachers 30 years earlier.

where do the rules come from?

Professional typography

Beyond that, lawyers have been known to be susceptible to boilerplate syndrome: the superstitious refusal to deviate from the form or substance of a document that was successfully used by another lawyer—usually sometime before the Carter administration.

It's not surprising that these bad habits get passed down. What's surprising is how tenacious they can be.

A core principle of this book is that typography in legal documents should be measured by the same standards as any professionally published material, like books, newspapers, and magazines. There is no "legal typography." There is only typography.

This wasn't always true. During the era when law offices relied on typewriters, professional publishers had typesetting and printing technology that was substantially better. So for lawyers, the typographic standards of professional publishers were far out of reach.

But that's no longer the case. Technology has brought law-office typesetting nearly up to the standards of professional typesetting. Modern word processors and laser printers have made it possible for lawyers to produce documents with excellent typography.

Therefore, lawyers should aspire to meet the standards of professional typography. That's why the rules here reflect the customs of professional typographers and the majority views of authorities on typography, filtered through my experience as a professional typographer and as a lawyer.

Must lawyers adopt every habit of professional typographers? No. I use professional typography as a benchmark for quality, not as an all-or-nothing goal. When faced with a choice between more consistency with professional typography or less, I believe lawyers should choose more consistency.

But I'm also a pragmatist. I know the feeling of rushing to finish a motion an hour before the deadline. I don't assume that lawyers have the time or interest to become professional typographers. I assume that your goal is to get the best typographic results for the lowest cost, and that nothing is more costly than your time. Therefore, I take a few shortcuts where the effort outweighs the results.

TOP   The keys of a manual typewriter.

BOTTOM The keyboard of a modern computer. Even though the computer keyboard can produce many more characters and symbols than the typewriter, much of that power is hidden from the writer.

Type composition

GOOD TYPOGRAPHY STARTS WITH good typing. This chapter is a tour of the non-alphabetic characters on the computer keyboard—some obscure, some underappreciated, and some well-known but misused.

A text is a sequence of characters. Every character is a tool. Your goal: to always use the right tool for the job.

Today's computer keyboards depict the available characters in almost the same way as a manual typewriter. But this depiction is misleading. The computer keyboard can produce many more characters than the ones visible on its keys. These include accented characters, symbols, and white-space characters—invisible markers that are useful for getting consistent typographic results.

Beware. This chapter is more difficult than it might seem. Typing is second nature for most of us. Habits are ingrained. After years of doing things one way, it can be hard to learn a different way.

But it's worth it. By typing the right characters while writing and editing, you'll save time and effort later on when you're formatting and laying out your document.

Basic rules

Straight quotes are the two generic vertical quotation marks located near the return key: the straight single quote (') and the straight double quote (").

Curly quotes are the quotation marks used in good typography. There are four curly quote characters: the opening single quote ('), the closing single quote ('), the opening double quote ("), and the closing double quote (").

On Windows, hold down the alt key and type the four-digit character code on your numeric keypad (num lock must be activated).

On the Mac, type the keys simultaneously.

		WINDOWS	MAC	HTML
'	straight single quote	'	'	'
"	straight double quote	"	"	"
'	opening single quote	*alt 0145*	*option +*]	&lsquo;
'	closing single quote	*alt 0146*	*option + shift +*]	&rsquo;
"	opening double quote	*alt 0147*	*option +* [	&ldquo;
"	closing double quote	*alt 0148*	*option + shift +* [	&rdquo;

Straight quotes come to us from the typewriter. In traditional printing, all quotation marks were curly. But typewriter character sets were limited by mechanical constraints and physical space. By replacing the curly opening and closing quotes with ambidextrous straight quotes, two slots became available for other characters.

Word processors are not limited in this way. You can always get curly quotes. Compared to straight quotes, curly quotes are more legible on the page and match the other characters better. Therefore, straight quotes should never, ever appear in your documents.

"That's a 'magic' sock." WRONG

"That's a 'magic' sock." RIGHT

Fortunately, avoiding straight quotes is easy: use your word processor's smart-quote feature, which will substitute curly quotes automatically. Smart quotes are typically turned on by default.

HOW TO TURN SMART QUOTES ON OR OFF

WORD 2003 | ‹Tools› → ‹AutoCorrect Options› → ‹AutoFormat As You Type› → *check or uncheck* ‹"Straight Quotes" with "Smart Quotes"›

WORD 2007 | *Office menu* → ‹Word Options› → ‹Proofing› → ‹AutoCorrect Options› → ‹AutoFormat As You Type› → *check or uncheck* ‹"Straight Quotes" with "Smart Quotes"›

WORD 2010 | ‹File› → ‹Options› → ‹Proofing› → ‹AutoCorrect Options› → ‹AutoFormat As You Type› → *check or uncheck* ‹"Straight Quotes" with "Smart Quotes"›

WORDPERFECT | ‹Tools› → ‹QuickCorrect› → ‹SmartQuotes› → *check or uncheck* ‹Use double quotation marks as you type› *and* ‹Use single quotation marks as you type›

PAGES | ‹Pages› → ‹Preferences› → ‹Auto-Correction› → *check or uncheck* ‹Use Smart Quotes (" ")›

Smart-quote substitution has been built into word processors for 20 years. That's why straight quotes are one of the most grievous and inept typographic errors.

So why do I keep seeing straight quotes in legal documents?

When you paste or import text with straight quotes in it—for instance, a deposition transcript or e-mail—your word processor may not always convert the straight quotes properly. Fix them.

One caveat: if you've corrected any APOSTROPHES that appear at the start of a word (**Patent '211**, **'70s rock**), this tip will goof them up again. So fix the quotes first, then the apostrophes.

HOW TO CONVERT ALL QUOTES TO CURLY QUOTES

1. Use the search-and-replace function to search for all instances of the straight single quote (') and replace it with the same character—a straight single quote (').

2. Use the search-and-replace function to search for all instances of the straight double quote (") and replace it with the same character—a straight double quote (").

Before you say "that won't do anything," try it. When your word processor replaces each quotation mark, it also performs the straight-to-curly conversion.

BY THE WAY

→ Straight quotes are acceptable in e-mail. It's hard to see the difference between straight and curly quotes on screen, at small sizes.

→ Some documents from online research services have double quotes made of two single quotes ('') or two grave accents (``). (The *grave accent*, also sometimes called a *backtick*, is that character above the tab key you've never used.) These can be fixed by adapting the search-and-replace technique described above.

→ Don't use quotation marks for emphasis.

→ Straight quotes in software code, including HTML, should not be converted to curly quotes. Those marks are part of the functional syntax of the code and should be reproduced literally.

Some topics in this book will offer you choices. Not this one.

Always put exactly one space between sentences.

Or more generally: put exactly one space after any punctuation.

Here's a paragraph with one space between sentences:

> I know that many people were taught to put two spaces between sentences. I was too. But these days, using two spaces is an obsolete habit. The practice was passed down from the typewriter era. Typewriter fonts had unusual proportions. Using two spaces helped set off sentences a bit better. We don't use typewriters anymore. So it's not standard. It's not part of typographic practice. Once in a while, you can use two spaces after sentences. When? If you're forced to use a typewriter-style font. These are also known as MONOSPACED FONTS.

Now the same paragraph, but with two spaces between sentences:

> I know that many people were taught to put two spaces between sentences. I was too. But these days, using two spaces is an obsolete habit. The practice was passed down from the typewriter era. Typewriter fonts had unusual proportions. Using two spaces helped set off sentences a bit better. We don't use typewriters anymore. So it's not standard. It's not part of typographic practice. Once in a while, you can use two spaces after sentences. When? If you're forced to use a typewriter-style font. These are also known as MONOSPACED FONTS.

See the problem? In the second paragraph, the extra spaces disrupt the balance of white space. Multiplied across a whole page, "rivers" of white space can appear.

one space between sentences

Always one — never two

And one more time, in a typewriter-style font, the one case where two spaces are tolerable (though still unnecessary):

```
I know that many people were taught to put two
spaces between sentences. I was too. But these
days, using two spaces is an obsolete habit. The
practice was passed down from the typewriter
era. Typewriter fonts had unusual proportions.
Using two spaces helped set off sentences a bit
better. We don't use typewriters anymore. So
it's not standard. It's not part of typographic
practice. Once in a while, you can use two spaces
after sentences. When? If you're forced to use
a typewriter-style font. These are also known as
monospaced fonts.
```

I have no idea why so many writers resist the one-space rule. If you're skeptical, pick up any book, newspaper, or magazine and tell me how many spaces there are between sentences.

Correct—one.

BY THE WAY

Still skeptical? You're not alone. For reasons unclear, this advice provokes unusual controversy. The objections sort out into these major themes:

You made up this so-called rule.

No. One space is the custom of professional typographers and the consensus view of typography authorities. No one has yet shown me contrary authority. For instance—

"Use a single word space between sentences. ... Your typing as well as your typesetting will benefit from unlearning [the] quaint Victorian habit" of using two spaces between sentences.

Robert Bringhurst, *The Elements of Typographic Style* (version 3.1), p. 28.

"[O]ne space between words and one space after punctuation marks (including colons and periods)."

Bryan A. Garner, *The Redbook: A Manual on Legal Style* (2nd ed.), p. 83.

"Chicago advises leaving a single character space, not two spaces, between sentences and after colons used within a sentence ... ."

The Chicago Manual of Style (16th ed.), rule 2.9.

That's fine for publications, but judges still prefer two spaces.

"Put only one space after punctuation. The typewriter convention of two spaces is for monospaced type only."

United States Court of Appeals for the Seventh Circuit, *Requirements and Suggestions for Typography in Briefs and Other Papers*, p. 5.

I think two spaces look better so that's what I'm going to use.

I'm telling you the rule. If you want to put personal taste ahead of the rule, I can't stop you. But personal taste does not neutralize the rule. It's like saying "I don't like how subjunctive-mood verbs sound, so I'm never going to use them."

I'm accustomed to seeing two spaces between sentences.

Are you? All the professionally typeset materials you read use one space between sentences.

Every lawyer I know uses two spaces.

A core principle of this book is that legal documents are governed by the same rules of typography as any professionally typeset book, newspaper, or magazine. If you agree, then the fact that lawyers habitually diverge from these rules is irrelevant. If you don't agree, consider giving this book to a friend.

Good arguments can be made for both options.

Except that it's not a matter of argument. One option has the support of typography authorities and professional practice; the other option does not. The issue is not ambiguous. Maybe in forty or fifty years, fashions will change. But that's a topic for the tenth edition of this book. For now—one space.

NOTE TO ARGUMENTATIVE READERS

Similar objections could be made against any rule in this book. This is the only time I will indulge them at length. These objections only serve to impede learning and preserve bad habits. If you're afflicted by the urge to protest, suppress it. That way, you can approach the rest of these rules with an open mind.

question marks and exclamation points

Ask more questions; avoid exclamations

The *question mark* is underused. Many times, you can make a legal issue simpler and pithier by presenting it in the form of a question. It's easy surgery:

This motion asks the Court to consider whether the statute of limitations is tolled by the fact that the defendant signed a waiver.   BEFORE

Does the defendant's signed waiver toll the statute of limitations?   AFTER

The *exclamation point* is overused. Give yourself a budget of one exclamation point for any document longer than three pages. If you must use it, use it wisely.

BY THE WAY

→ In traditional print shops, an exclamation point was also known as a *bang*. The combination of a question mark and exclamation point (?!)—seen mostly in dialogue balloons in comics—is called an *interrobang*. An interrobang LIGATURE was invented in 1962 and has had an undistinguished career.

interrobang
ligature

→ Never use more than one exclamation point in a row, unless you're a teenager sending a text message.

The *semicolon* (;) has two primary uses.

(1) It's used instead of a conjunction to combine two sentences (*He did the crime; he must do the time*). Don't use a semicolon to connect a subordinate clause to a sentence (*Since he did the crime; he must do the time*). In that case, use a comma.

In a sentence with a conjunction, don't use a semicolon before the conjunction (*He did the crime; and he must do the time*). Use either a comma or no punctuation before the conjunction. Or start a new sentence at the conjunction.

(2) A semicolon also separates list elements with internal commas (*We visited Tulsa, Oklahoma; Flint, Michigan; and Paducah, Kentucky*).

The *colon* (:) usually connects the introduction of an idea and its completion (*I own three cars: a convertible, a sedan, and a minivan*).

Semicolons are often mistakenly used where a colon is correct, and vice versa. Make sure you've got the right one.

semicolons and colons

Don't mix them up

Exceptions exist. For comprehensive explanations, consult *Garner's Modern American Usage* (see BIBLIOGRAPHY), the authority on how to use semicolons, colons, other punctuation marks, and the rest of the English language.

*Add a
nonbreaking
space*

The *paragraph mark* (¶) is used when citing documents with sequentially numbered paragraphs (e.g., declarations or complaints). The *section mark* (§) is used when citing documents with numbered or lettered sections (e.g., statutes).

		WINDOWS	MAC	HTML
¶	paragraph mark	*alt 0182*	*option + 7*	*¶*
§	section mark	*alt 0167*	*option + 6*	*§*

A paragraph mark or section mark should always be followed by a NONBREAKING SPACE. The nonbreaking space acts like glue that keeps the mark joined with the numeric reference that follows.

Without the nonbreaking space, the mark and the reference can end up on separate lines or pages. This can confuse readers.

> The defendant has the option under Civil Code §
> 1782 to offer a correction to affected buyers. But ¶
> 17 of the agreement suggests it is required.   WRONG

> The defendant has the option under Civil Code
> § 1782 to offer a correction to affected buyers. But
> ¶ 17 of the agreement suggests it is required.   RIGHT

If the paragraph or section reference comes at the start of a sentence, don't use the mark—spell out the whole word (*Section 17200 applied to the transaction, but § 17500 did not*). In a reference to multiple paragraphs or sections, double the mark (¶¶ or §§).

Citation formats for rules (e.g., the Federal Rules of Evidence, rules of court, rules of professional conduct) don't usually call for a section mark (*Fed. R. Evid. 801*, not *Fed. R. Evid. § 801*).

➡ The paragraph mark is also known as a *pilcrow*.

➡ Your citation guide may have more to say about this topic. For instance, the *California Style Manual* does not permit section marks outside parenthetical citations—you have to spell out the whole word.

A rare instance where common usage and legal usage are almost the same. *Parentheses* are for separating citations or other asides. *Brackets* show changes to quoted material. *Braces* are not typically used.

(parentheses) [brackets] {braces}

Some citation guides, including the *California Style Manual*, demand brackets for parallel citations.

> "*Bertero* was not meant to discourage [the] practice [of pleading alternative legal theories]." (*Crowley v. Katleman* (1994) 8 Cal.4th 666, 691 [881 P.2d 1083, 34 Cal.Rptr.2d 386].)   RIGHT

➡ Why do braces still get prime real estate on keyboards? They're part of the syntax of nearly every software-programming language. You may not use braces, but modern life wouldn't be possible without them.

parentheses, brackets, and braces

Stay the course

The **California Style Manual** is an alternative citation system used in California state courts in slight preference to the *Bluebook* (though *Bluebook*-style citations are also accepted).

hyphens and dashes

Use them, don't confuse them

Hyphens and dashes look similar, but they're not interchangeable.

		WINDOWS	MAC	HTML
-	hyphen	-	-	-
—	en dash	*alt 0150*	*option + hyphen*	*–*
——	em dash	*alt 0151*	*option + shift + hyphen*	*—*

The *hyphen* (-) is the smallest of these marks. It has three uses.

①　A hyphen appears at the end of a line when a word breaks onto the next line. These hyphens are added and removed automatically by your word processor's HYPHENATION feature.

②　Some multipart words are spelled with a hyphen (*topsy-turvy, cost-effective, bric-a-brac*). But a prefix is not typically followed with a hyphen (*nonprofit*, not *non-profit*).

③　A hyphen is used in phrasal adjectives (*commercial-speech restriction, estate-planning attorney, law-school grades*) to ensure clarity. Nonprofessional writers often omit these hyphens. As a professional writer, you should not.

No hyphen is necessary in phrasal adjectives that begin with an adverb ending in **-ly** (it's a **closely held company**, not a **closely-held company**). Nor is a hyphen necessary in multipart foreign terms or proper names used as adjectives (**habeas corpus appeal on the Third Circuit docket**, not **habeas-corpus appeal on the Third-Circuit docket**).

For instance, consider the unhyphenated phrase *five dollar bills*. Is *five* the quantity of *dollar bills*, or are the *bills* each worth *five dollars*? As written, it suggests the former. If you mean the latter, then you'd write *five-dollar bills*.

Dashes come in two sizes—the *en dash* and the *em dash*. The em dash (—) is typically about as wide as a capital H. The en dash (–) is about half as wide.

En and em dashes are often approximated by typing two or three hyphens in a row (-- or ---). Don't do that. Use real dashes.

The en dash has two uses.

(1) It indicates a range of values (*1880–1912, 116 Cal. App. 4th 330–39, Exhibits A–E*). If you open with *from*, pair it with *to* instead of an en dash (*from 1880 to 1912*, not *from 1880–1912*).

(2) It denotes a connection or contrast between pairs of words (*conservative–liberal split, Arizona–Nevada reciprocity, Sarbanes–Oxley Act*).

Don't use a slash (/) where an en dash is correct.

Be careful when citing a source like *Local Rule 7-3*. That gets a hyphen, not an en dash, because it's the multipart name of a single rule, not a range of rules.

The em dash is used to make a break between parts of a sentence. Use it when a comma is too weak, but a colon, semicolon, or pair of parentheses is too strong. The em dash puts a nice pause in the text—and it is underused in legal writing.

BY THE WAY

➡ Even though the en dash is used for joint authors (*Sarbanes–Oxley Act*), use a hyphen for compound names. If the children of Sarbanes and Oxley married, they'd be known as *Mr. & Mrs. Sarbanes-Oxley* (with a hyphen), not *Mr. & Mrs. Sarbanes–Oxley* (with an en dash).

➡ Em and en dashes are typically set flush against the surrounding text. Some fonts include a little white space around the em dash; some don't. If your em dashes look like they're being crushed, it's fine to add WORD SPACES before and after.

➡ An en dash makes an acceptable minus sign in spreadsheets or mathematical expressions. (See also MATH SYMBOLS.)

➡ *Em* and *en* refer to units of typographic measurement, not to the letters M and N. In a traditional metal font, the em was the vertical distance from the top of a piece of type to the bottom. The en was half the size of the em. Originally, the width of the em and en dashes corresponded to these units. In today's digital fonts, they run narrower.

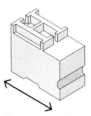

the **em** on a piece of metal type

trademark and copyright symbols

Don't use alphabetic substitutes

Your keyboard includes a *trademark symbol* (™), a *registered trademark symbol* (®), and a *copyright symbol* (©).

		WINDOWS	MAC	HTML
TM	trademark	*alt 0153*	*option + 2*	*™*
®	registered trademark	*alt 0174*	*option + r*	*®*
©	copyright	*alt 0169*	*option + g*	*©*

Use these symbols when you need them. Don't use alphabetic approximations like *(TM)* or *(c)*.

(c) 2013 MegaCorp (TM)   WRONG
© 2013 MegaCorp™   RIGHT

Trademark symbols are set as superscripts—smaller characters positioned above the baseline of the text (*Roxy's Pizza*™, *Caring Is Our Business*®). If you use proper trademark symbols, they'll appear at the right size and height. No space is needed between the text and the trademark symbol.

Copyright symbols appear in line with the text (© *1999*). Use a NONBREAKING SPACE between the copyright symbol and the year to ensure the two don't end up on different lines or pages.

This instructional goatherding video is © 2013 MegaCorp Inc.   WRONG

This instructional goatherding video is © 2013 MegaCorp Inc.   RIGHT

Must you put a word space after the copyright symbol? No, but semantically, it makes good sense. The © directly replaces the word *copyright*, so it should be spaced like any other word. Trademark symbols, on the other hand, are more like little barnacles of legalese—immovable but mostly ignored. To think of it another way, if you were reading the phrase "© 2013 MegaCorp™" aloud, you'd probably pronounce the © but not the ™.

BY THE WAY

→ Some word processors automatically substitute a symbol when you type (TM), (R), or (c). Be cautious with this feature, because citations like *Fed. R. Civ. P. 12(c)* can be silently converted to *Fed. R. Civ. P. 12©*. The spelling checker won't detect this error and it's easy to overlook while editing.

→ *Copyright © 2013* is redundant. Word or symbol—not both.

→ To dispel an urban legend that persists among many civilians, and more than a few lawyers: with respect to newly created works, the copyright symbol has no magic powers. Putting a copyright symbol on something you made does not grant you a copyright. Nor does failing to use it deprive you of a copyright.

→ I always use the nonitalicized versions of these marks, even if the adjacent text is italicized. I think it looks better. But that's a preference, not a rule.

ampersands

Use sparingly

The *ampersand* is typographic shorthand for the word *and*. The ampersand is halfway between a LIGATURE and a contraction, a stylized depiction of the Latin word *et*.

The ampersand is one of the jauntiest characters. Font designers often use it as an opportunity to show off. Traditional ampersands take the shape of the word *et*. Modern ampersands are more stylized.

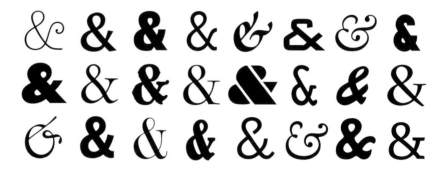

Ampersands are completely correct when they're part of a proper name (*Fromage & Cracotte LLP*) or an official citation format (*Bus. & Prof. Code § 17200*).

Past that, ampersands should be handled like any other contraction: the more formal the document, the more sparingly they should be used. Here and there, but not everywhere.

An *ellipsis* (plural *ellipses*) is a sequence of three dots used to indicate an omission in quoted material.

		WINDOWS	MAC	HTML
•••	ellipsis	*alt 0133*	*option + semicolon*	*…*

The ellipsis is frequently approximated by typing three periods in a row, which puts the dots too close together, or three periods with spaces in between, which puts the dots too far apart.

So use the ellipsis character, not the approximations.

from a ... to z   WRONG

from a . . . to z   WRONG

from a ... to z   RIGHT

Should you put WORD SPACES around an ellipsis? As with the em dash (see HYPHENS AND DASHES), that's up to you. Typically you'll want spaces before and after, but if that looks odd, you can take them out. If there's text on only one side of the ellipsis, use a NONBREAKING SPACE on that side so the ellipsis doesn't get separated from the text.

BLUEBOOK ELLIPSES

Bluebook rule 5.3 (19th ed. 2010) demands ellipses that look like periods with word spaces between them and around them.

imperative to . . . courts   RIGHT

The problem with using periods and word spaces is that it invites your word processor to break the ellipsis across different lines or pages, like so:

imperative to . .
. courts

To keep the dots together, make a *Bluebook* ellipsis out of three periods with NONBREAKING SPACES in between. Also use nonbreaking spaces on the ends unless there's text on both sides. This ensures the periods will behave like a single unit of punctuation.

When the *Bluebook* calls for a four-dot sequence, build it the same way as a three-dot ellipsis—as four periods with nonbreaking spaces in between.

BY THE WAY

→ I sometimes wonder whether the zigzagging illogic of the *Bluebook* is calculated to protect its franchise—after all, if legal citation were distilled to a few simple rules, no one would need the *Bluebook*. Its subtitle—"A Uniform System of Citation"—compresses a lot of dark humor into five words.

The problem with the *Bluebook*'s four-dot-sequence rules is that they use the same visual mark—four periods separated by spaces—to denote at least four distinct conditions. Namely: a deletion before a sentence-ending period (rule 5.3(b)(iii)); a sentence-ending period before a deletion (rule 5.3(b)(v)); a deletion both at the end and after the end of a sentence (rule 5.3(b)(vi)); and a deletion of one or more paragraphs (rule 5.1(a)(iii)). This invites ambiguity. When readers come upon a four-dot sequence, how do they know what it signifies? It may not be clear from context. Proper ellipses would help distinguish these conditions.

TYPE COMPOSITION

A *signature line* is a horizontal line aligned with adjacent text.

signature lines

Type a sequence of underscores

Typography purists avoid accomplishing anything by holding down keys on the keyboard. But in this case it's the simplest solution. To make a signature line, hold down the underscore key (shift + hyphen) until you get the length you need.

_____

A rival school of thought suggests you should type a series of WORD SPACES and format them with UNDERLINING.

_____

Same thing, right? Not quite. There are three good reasons to prefer underscores to underlined word spaces.

To make a signature block that won't break across pages, see KEEP LINES TOGETHER.

1. If you need to quickly rid a document of UNDERLINING, you might want to select all the text and then uncheck the underlining option. But this will wreck signature lines made out of underlined word spaces—they will disappear.

2. If you need to quickly ensure you only have ONE SPACE BETWEEN SENTENCES, you might want to search for and replace any double spaces. But this will also wreck signature lines made out of word spaces—by partially deleting them.

3. Underscore characters don't depend on formatting, so they will look the same no matter where they're copied and pasted. Underlined word spaces may not.

You should depart from this rule only if the font you're using has an underscore character that doesn't form a solid line when used in sequence. That's how underscores are supposed to work, but some fonts are defective. Sometimes the gaps only appear on screen, so print a test page. If the gaps appear in print too, use underlined word spaces instead.

Advanced rules

apostrophes

*Make sure
they're curly
and point
downward*

The *apostrophe* has two functions we all remember from sixth-grade English class.

① An apostrophe indicates the possessive case (*Jessica's bagel*).

② In contractions, an apostrophe takes the place of letters or numbers that have been removed (*is not* becomes *isn't*, *Patent No. 5,269,211* becomes *'211*).

Apostrophes always point downward. If the smart-quote feature of your word processor is on (see STRAIGHT AND CURLY QUOTES), then type an apostrophe with the same key you use to type a straight single quote ('). Your word processor will convert this character to a curly apostrophe ('). Or you can type an apostrophe directly, using the same key as a closing single quote.

		WINDOWS	MAC	HTML
'	straight single quote	'	'	'
'	apostrophe (same as closing single quote)	*alt 0146*	*option + shift +]*	&rsquo;

Text imported from a plain-text source (e.g., a deposition transcript or e-mail) may not have its apostrophes converted to curly apostrophes. To fix this, use the search-and-replace technique in STRAIGHT AND CURLY QUOTES.

Wrinkles arise when an apostrophe is used at the beginning of a word (again, assuming your smart-quote feature is on). If you type the phrase:

In the '60s, rock 'n' roll

No, you don't need an apostrophe before the **s** in **'60s**.

This will be displayed as:

In the '60s, rock 'n' roll   WRONG

The problem here is that the characters in front of *60s* and *n'* aren't apostrophes—they're opening single quotes. They point upward. What you need is an apostrophe in place of each sequence of omitted letters, so the result looks like this:

In the '60s, rock 'n' roll   RIGHT

To get this result, you have two choices. You can manually delete the incorrect marks and type apostrophes directly. Or you can type straight single quotes twice:

In the ''60s, rock ''n' roll

Word has its own apostrophe shortcut—hold down the control key and type the straight single quote twice.

These will be displayed as:

In the ''60s, rock ''n' roll

Then you can delete the unneeded opening single quotes, getting you back to:

In the '60s, rock 'n' roll   RIGHT

→   If you're using Hawaiian spellings of Hawaiian words, look out. Those apostrophe-like characters aren't apostrophes—they're *okinas*. The okina is a letter in the Hawaiian alphabet that doesn't exist in English. Okinas point upward, so use an opening single quote as your okina, not an apostrophe. If the okina appears in the middle of a word, your word processor will incorrectly insert an apostrophe.

Hawai'i   O'ahu's   WRONG
Hawaiʻi   Oʻahu's   RIGHT

Alternatively, you can omit the okinas. Anglicized spellings of Hawaiian words are almost always acceptable.

Hawaii   Oahu's   RIGHT

The okina is a *glottal stop*. In English, the glottal stop is heard before some vowels, like in the middle of the word *uh-oh*.

I assume you're writing in American English, but you might still encounter *accented characters* in foreign words. Foreign words arise in two situations:

① In proper names, like people and places (*Albrecht Dürer, François Truffaut, Plácido Domingo*). In names, accented characters must always appear accurately. Otherwise, the name is misspelled.

② In loanwords used in American English. Some of these words have become naturalized citizens and should be spelled without accents (*naive* for *naïve, melee* for *mêlée, coupe* for *coupé*). Others have not and should not (*cause célèbre, piña colada, Götterdämmerung*). Check a dictionary or usage guide.

The inside back cover of this book has a table of the most common accented characters and how to type them.

BY THE WAY

➥ Proper names are not italicized, but loanwords sometimes are, depending on their degree of assimilation. Again, check a dictionary or usage guide.

➥ The German letter *Eszett* is technically a LIGATURE, not an accented character: it takes the place of *ss* in a word like *Straße*. Unlike ligatures in English, its use in German is not discretionary—Germany has adopted rules for when it must appear and when it must not. (To the surprise of no one.) Switzerland, meanwhile, disregards the Eszett, and just uses *ss*. And almost no one uses the Eszett with ALL CAPS. So it's best to follow Switzerland's lead and ignore it. Even if you place the Eszett correctly, it's less common to English speakers than the usual accented characters, and it can easily be mistaken for a letter *B* or a Greek beta (β). If you really must type one, on Windows it's alt 0223; on the Mac it's option+s.

Eszett

foot and inch marks

Use straight quotes, not curly

Foot and inch marks—also known as minute and second marks or prime and double prime marks, depending on what they're labeling—are not curly. Use straight quotes for these marks.

		WINDOWS	MAC	HTML
'	foot mark	'	'	'
"	inch mark	"	"	"

"But back in STRAIGHT AND CURLY QUOTES, you told me to turn on smart quotes. So now, when I try to type foot and inch marks, they come out curly, not straight." A fair point.

HOW TO OVERRIDE SMART QUOTES

WORD | *Type the foot or inch mark, which will come out curly, and then press control + z (undo). The curly mark will become straight.*

WORDPERFECT | *No special action necessary. After numbers, WordPerfect overrides smart quotes and inserts straight quotes.*

PAGES | *‹Edit› → ‹Special Characters› → ‹Punctuation›. In the search box at the bottom, enter ‹apostrophe› for the foot mark or ‹quotation mark› for the inch mark and press enter. The mark will be highlighted in the window above. Drag the mark into your text. Don't double-click, or it will be inserted as a curly mark.*

5' 6"

angled foot and inch marks

Typography purists would point out that proper foot and inch marks have a slight northeast-to-southwest slope to them. True, but those characters aren't available in most fonts. So straight quotes are the most reliable tools for the job.

–118° 19' 36.9" WRONG

–118° 19' 36.9" RIGHT

You can italicize the straight quotes if you want an even better approximation of sloped foot and inch marks.

−118° 19′ 36.9″   BONUS POINTS

Tread carefully if foot and inch marks appear within quoted material.

"She's 6' 10"."   WRONG

"She's 6' 10"."   HOPELESS

"She's 6' 10"."   RIGHT

BY THE WAY

➜ A NONBREAKING SPACE in the middle of a foot-and-inch measurement will prevent it from splitting onto the next line. So instead of *6′ 10″*, you'll get *6′ 10″*.

---

white-space characters

For control and predictability

You're now familiar with the essential alphabetic, numeric, and symbol characters. We turn to the frequently overlooked *white-space characters*—the keyboard characters that put blank space between point A and point B.

Why are they overlooked? For one thing, they're invisible.

HOW TO DISPLAY WHITE-SPACE CHARACTERS

WORD 2003 | ‹¶› *button on the standard toolbar (or control + shift + 8)*

WORD 2007 & 2010 | ‹Home› ➜ ‹Paragraph› *panel* ➜ ‹¶› *button (or control + shift + 8)*

If I have to work on a document from an outside source, one of the first things I do is display white-space characters, to uncover lurking horrors.

As you learn to use white-space characters, you'll find it helpful to make them visible so you can verify that you're typing them correctly and that they're having the intended effect. After you're proficient, you'll find it useful to see the white-space characters while diagnosing formatting problems.

There are six important white-space characters: the WORD SPACE, the NONBREAKING SPACE, the TAB, the HARD LINE BREAK, the CARRIAGE RETURN, and the HARD PAGE BREAK. Each white-space character has a distinct function. Use the right tool for the job.

"But if all white space looks the same when printed, why should I care?" Two reasons: *control* and *predictability*.

Control means you get the intended result with the minimum keystrokes. Suppose you need a paragraph to start at the top of the next page. What do you do? If you use a hard page break rather than a sequence of carriage returns, you get the job done with one keystroke.

Predictability means that as you edit and reformat, you'll always get the same result. If you approximate a hard page break with carriage returns, at some point in your editing, your text will reflow and you'll have a large, unexpected gap where you intended a page break. Then you'll have a new problem to diagnose and fix. But a hard page break will always do the right thing.

The time you invest in learning how to use white-space characters will be paid back in layouts that come together faster and require less maintenance.

The *word space* has exactly one purpose: to create horizontal clearance between two words. Likewise, the space bar has exactly one purpose: to insert a single word space.

	WORD	**WORDPERFECT**	**PAGES**
word space	*space bar*	*space bar*	*space bar*

Don't use the space bar as a general-purpose white-space dispenser by holding it down and watching the cursor glide across the screen. Though it may be a calming sight, it leads to anguish when formatting the document. Use exactly one word space at a time.

Your word processor assumes that a word space marks a safe place to flow text onto a new line or page. A *nonbreaking space* is the same width as a word space, but it prevents the text from flowing to a new line or page. It's like invisible glue between the words on either side.

	WORD	**WORDPERFECT**	**PAGES**
nonbreaking space	*control + shift + space bar*	*control + space bar*	*option + shift + space bar*

Put a nonbreaking space before any numeric or alphabetic reference to prevent awkward breaks. Recall this example from PARAGRAPH AND SECTION MARKS:

> The defendant has the option under Civil Code §
> 1782 to offer a correction to affected buyers. But ¶
> 17 of the agreement suggests it is required.   WRONG

> The defendant has the option under Civil Code
> § 1782 to offer a correction to affected buyers. But
> ¶ 17 of the agreement suggests it is required.   RIGHT

In the top example, normal word spaces come after the § and ¶ symbols, and the numeric references incorrectly appear on the next line.

In the bottom example, nonbreaking spaces come after the § and ¶ symbols. This time, the symbols and the numeric references stay together.

Use nonbreaking spaces after other abbreviated reference marks (*Ex. A*, *Fig. 23*), after copyright symbols (see TRADEMARK AND COPYRIGHT SYMBOLS), and between the dots in *Bluebook*-compliant ELLIPSES.

In citations, use your judgment. In the citation *Fed. R. Evid. 702*, you can put a nonbreaking space before the *702* so it won't get separated from *Evid*. But certain citation formats, like the *California Style Manual*, don't use spaces in the abbreviated name of the source (*116 Cal.App.4th 602*). In those cases, the nonbreaking space can cause more problems than it solves, because it creates a large, unbreakable chunk of letters.

tabs and tab stops

For horizontal space in the middle of a line

On typewriters, the *tab* key moved the carriage to a fixed horizontal position, marked with a *tab stop*. This allowed typists to create columns of text or numbers, also known as tabular layouts (hence the name *tab*).

Tabs and tab stops still work the same way. A tab stop marks a location; typing a tab moves the cursor to that location.

	WORD	WORDPERFECT	PAGES
tab	*tab*	*tab*	*tab*

These days, the tab is used only for inserting horizontal space in the middle of a line. If you need horizontal space at the beginning of a paragraph, adjust the FIRST-LINE INDENT. For a true tabular layout, use a TABLE, not tabs.

The tab is not as vital as it once was, but word processors still short change its capabilities. A new word-processing document has default tab stops every half inch. These default tab stops exist so that something happens when you type a tab in the new document. But this default behavior also suggests that what the tab key does is move the cursor a half inch at a time. Not true.

To get the most out of tabs, you should set your own tab stops. Avoid relying on the default tab stops—they undermine the goals of control and predictability. As with WORD SPACES, also avoid using sequences of tabs to move the cursor around the screen.

WordPerfect displays its default tab stops on its ruler. Word and Pages do not (for no good reason). In Word and Pages, be aware that adding your own tab stops wipes out the default ones. So you'll usually want to set tab stops before inserting tabs in the text.

To see your tab stops, display the ruler.

HOW TO DISPLAY THE RULER

WORD 2003 | ‹View› ➡ ‹Ruler›

WORD 2007 | ‹View› ➡ ‹Show/Hide› *panel* ➡ ‹Ruler›

WORD 2010 | ‹View› ➡ ‹Show› *panel* ➡ ‹Ruler›

WORDPERFECT | ‹View› ➡ ‹Ruler›, *or type alt + shift + F3*

PAGES | ‹View› ➡ ‹Show Rulers›, *or type command + r*

With the ruler visible, you can edit your tab stops.

HOW TO WORK WITH TAB STOPS

① To insert a new tab stop, click in the ruler where you want the tab stop.

② To move a tab stop, click and drag it in the ruler.

③ To change a tab stop from one kind to another, double-click it in the ruler. In WordPerfect and Pages, you can also right-click it.

④ To remove a tab stop, drag it off the ruler.

Many layout tasks traditionally handled by tabs are now better handled by tables. For instance, this illustration of tab stops was made with tabs, but it would've been easier to use a four-column, four-row table.

The usual tab stop is a left tab stop, meaning text under the tab stop aligns to its left edges. Word processors also offer center and right tab stops, having the expected effects, as well as decimal tab stops that align columns of numbers along their decimal points.

This	This	$1234.56	This
is a	is a	78.9%	is a
left tab	centered tab	decimal.tab	right tab
stop	stop	st.op	stop

Use the proper tab stop for the job. For instance, don't use a center tab stop to line up decimal numbers. A right tab can be useful in a document footer to put two pieces of text (e.g., the document title and the page number) at opposite ends of the same line.

Despite their names, automatic tables of contents and tables of authorities are not made with true word-processor tables. If you want to edit them, you need to be comfortable adjusting tab stops.

Tabs are used in BULLETED AND NUMBERED LISTS to separate the bullet or number from the text. Tabs are also used in automatically generated tables of contents and tables of authorities to put the page numbers at the right edge of the table.

Tabs and tab stops have their place, but in most cases they act as a less-capable alternative to a table. Use tabs and tab stops if your formatting task is truly simple. If not, upgrade to a table.

BY THE WAY

➜ You can fill the space in front of a tab (for instance, with periods or underscores) by using a *tab leader*. Don't approximate this effect by typing a hundred periods or underscores manually in front of a tab. That will lead to unpleasant consequences.

The *hard line break* moves the next word to the beginning of a new line without starting a new paragraph.

	WORD	WORDPERFECT	PAGES
hard line break	*shift + enter*	*control + shift + L*	*shift + enter*

A hard line break can help control text flow when a CARRIAGE RETURN won't work. For instance, this HEADING breaks awkwardly:

IV. **The defendant is entitled to judgment as a matter of law.**

Suppose you want the line to break after *judgment* so the first line ends in a more logical place and the two lines are better balanced. If you use a CARRIAGE RETURN, you'll get:

IV. **The defendant is entitled to judgment**

V. **as a matter of law.** WRONG

Not what you want. Instead, put a hard line break after *judgment*:

IV. **The defendant is entitled to judgment as a matter of law.** RIGHT

Hard line breaks are also useful for separating the lines of an address (for instance, on LETTERHEAD or a CAPTION PAGE). See CENTERED TEXT for another example of the hard line break in use.

carriage returns

Only when you want a new paragraph

On manual typewriters, the *carriage* was the cylinder that held the paper and scooted leftward as you typed. At the end of each line, you'd push a lever to move the carriage to the beginning of the next line. On electric typewriters, this lever became the *carriage return* key, which you'd use at the end of each line.

The terminology has stayed with us, but on a word processor, you only use a carriage return to start a new paragraph.

	WORD	WORDPERFECT	PAGES
carriage return	*enter*	*enter*	*enter*

In e-mail, it's fine to use multiple carriage returns to add vertical space, because there's no other way to do it.

As with the WORD SPACE, use only one carriage return at a time. It's common to see multiple carriage returns used to add vertical space between paragraphs. Bad idea. If you want vertical space after a paragraph, use SPACE BETWEEN PARAGRAPHS.

"But it's so much easier to type two carriage returns." I know. But in long, structured documents, extra carriage returns create unpredictable consequences as the document is edited. Whatever time you save with the shortcut will cost you later.

What if you get a document that's already littered with double carriage returns? Search-and-replace works with WHITE-SPACE CHARACTERS too.

HOW TO REPLACE DOUBLE CARRIAGE RETURNS

WORD 2003 & 2007 | ‹Find and Replace› *(control + f)* ➔ ‹Replace› ➔ ‹More›. *Use the* ‹Special› *menu to put two* ‹Paragraph Marks› *in the* ‹Find what› *box, and one* ‹Paragraph Mark› *in the* ‹Replace with› *box. (Careful: you don't want the* ‹Paragraph Character›, *which denotes the literal* ¶ *symbol.) Click* ‹Replace All›.

WORD 2010 | *Open* ‹Find and Replace› *with control + g, then continue as described above.*

WORDPERFECT | ‹Find and Replace› *(control + f)* ➞ ‹Match› ➞ ‹Codes›. *Scroll down to the code* ‹HRt›. *(*‹HRt› *is short for "hard return," WordPerfect's term for a carriage return.) Put two* ‹HRt›*s in the* ‹Replace› *box and one in the* ‹Replace with› *box. Click* ‹Replace All›.

PAGES | ‹Find & Replace› *(command + f)* ➞ ‹Advanced›. *Use the* ‹Insert› *popup menu next to the* ‹Find› *box to insert two* ‹Paragraph Breaks›. *Use the* ‹Insert› *popup menu next to the* ‹Replace› *box to insert one* ‹Paragraph Break›. *(There's also a character on the* ‹Insert› *popup menu called* ‹Carriage Return›. *Don't use this—it won't have the intended effect.) Click* ‹Replace All›.

The *hard page break* puts the next word at the top of a new page.

	WORD	WORDPERFECT	PAGES
hard page break	*control + enter*	*control + enter*	*control + num-pad enter*

To move text to the next page, use one hard page break, not multiple CARRIAGE RETURNS. If you use carriage returns, your document will become impossible to edit—as soon as you change anything before the page break, the text will go out of alignment. The hard page break guarantees consistent behavior.

HOW TO INSERT A HARD PAGE BREAK (ALTERNATE METHOD)

WORD 2003 | ‹Insert› ➞ ‹Break› ➞ ‹Page Break›

WORD 2007 & 2010 | ‹Page Layout› ➞ ‹Page Setup› *panel* ➞ ‹Breaks› ➞ ‹Page›, *or* ‹Insert› ➞ ‹Pages› *panel* ➞ ‹Page Break›

WORDPERFECT | ‹Insert› ➞ ‹New Page›

PAGES | ‹Insert› ➞ ‹Page Break›

hard page breaks

Move to the top of the next page

➤ If you use a hard page break, don't fill the blank lines on the previous page with slashes. It's a meaningless and obsolete ritual.

/ /
/ /
/ /

I theorize that this habit descended from some early digital word-processing system that used two slashes to signal a new line. I don't know for sure. It doesn't matter. What matters is that you stop. The slashes look bad and they create needless cleanup work every time you edit the document and the location of the page break changes.

➤ Hard page breaks can be built into paragraph styles to ensure that classes of paragraphs (e.g., major section headings) always start at the top of a new page. See PAGE BREAK BEFORE.

nonbreaking hyphens

Hyphens that act like nonbreaking spaces

Your word processor assumes that any hyphen marks a safe place to flow the text onto a new line or page. Similar to the NONBREAKING SPACE, the *nonbreaking hyphen* looks identical to a hyphen but will not be used as a place for a line break or page break.

	WORD	**WORDPERFECT**	**PAGES**
nonbreaking hyphen	*control + shift + hyphen*	*control + hyphen*	*see below*

To what end? A nonbreaking hyphen guards against an awkward line break in a citation with an internal hyphen.

The meeting required by Local Rule 7-3 was scheduled for July 15, 2009.   WRONG

The meeting required by Local Rule 7-3 was scheduled for July 15, 2009.   RIGHT

HOW TO INSERT A NONBREAKING HYPHEN IN PAGES

PAGES | ‹Edit› ➡ ‹Special Characters›. *Using the box at the bottom of the window, search for "non-breaking hyphen," which will bring up the character.*

The *optional hyphen* is usually invisible. The optional hyphen marks where a word should be hyphenated if the word lands at the end of a line. You can put multiple optional hyphens in a word.

Why would you want to do this? Some words bedevil hyphenation engines. For instance, *TrueType* will often get hyphenated as *Tru-eType*. To prevent this, I put an optional hyphen in the middle (*True~Type*) so it will be hyphenated correctly.

How do you know whether a word won't be hyphenated correct-ly? The problem usually afflicts words that aren't in a standard hy-phenation dictionary, like jargon words, unusual proper names, and other words with nonstandard spellings, like trade names. As Jus-tice Potter Stewart might have said, you'll know it when you see it.

optional hyphens

Mark a hyphenation location

HOW TO INSERT AN OPTIONAL HYPHEN

WORD 2003 | ‹Insert› ➡ ‹Symbol› ➡ ‹Special Characters› ➡ ‹Optional Hyphen›

WORD 2007 & 2010 | ‹Insert› ➡ ‹Symbols› *panel* ➡ ‹Symbol› ➡ ‹More Symbols› ➡ ‹Special Characters› ➡ ‹Optional Hyphen›

WORDPERFECT | ‹Format› ➡ ‹Line› ➡ ‹Other Codes› ➡ ‹Soft hyphen›

PAGES | *Not available*

BY THE WAY

➡ Remember, even though you type a key to insert an optional hyphen, you won't see it until it's needed.

math symbols

Use real symbols, not alphabetic characters

If you need *math symbols* infrequently—some light addition and subtraction, the occasional negative number—you can get by without special symbols. Use the plus sign (+) and equals sign (=) as usual. Use the en dash as a minus sign (–) (see HYPHENS AND DASHES).

If you need to do multiplication or beyond, insert real math symbols by hand.

$$123 \text{ x } 345 - 678 = 41757 \quad \text{WRONG}$$

$$123 \times 345 - 678 = 41757 \quad \text{RIGHT}$$

HOW TO INSERT MATH SYMBOLS

WORD 2003 | ‹Insert› → ‹Symbol›. *From the ‹Font› popup menu, select ‹Symbol›. From the character palette that appears, double-click the symbol you want.*

WORD 2007 & 2010 | ‹Insert› → ‹Symbols› *panel* → ‹Symbol› → ‹More Symbols›. *From the ‹Font› popup menu, select ‹Symbol›. From the character palette that appears, double-click the symbol you want.*

WORDPERFECT | ‹Insert› → ‹Symbol›. *From the ‹Set› popup menu, select ‹Math / Scientific›. From the character palette that appears, double-click the symbol you want.*

PAGES | ‹Edit› → ‹Special Characters›. *In the scrolling list on the left, go to ‹Symbols› → ‹Mathematical Symbols›. From the character palette that appears, double-click the symbol you want.*

BY THE WAY

→ The multiplication symbol is also properly part of dimensional notations like *8.5″ × 14″* (not *8.5″x 14″*).

Ligatures were invented to solve a practical typesetting problem. In the days of metal fonts, certain characters had features that physically collided with other characters. To fix this, font makers included ligatures with their fonts, which combined the troublesome letters into one piece of type.

The most common ligatures involve the lowercase f because of its unique geometry. Other ligatures also exist—some practical, some decorative.

ff fi fj ffl Th   NO LIGATURES

ff fi fj ffl Th   LIGATURES

Most digital fonts are designed so that characters don't collide. Therefore, ligatures don't serve the practical purpose they once did. To my eye, ligatures bestow a slightly quaint or old-fashioned look on modern documents.

If you like that look, great. Use all the ligatures you want.

I don't like that look. So I turn off ligatures unless there's an actual collision between the letters f and i. Check this combination in the bold and italic styles too.

fi fi *fi* fi **fi**   RIGHT

fi *fi* fi fi **fi**   WRONG

fi *fi* fi fi **fi**   RIGHT

The fonts in the first row above have fi combinations that don't collide. Those fonts will work fine without ligatures. But the fonts in the second row have fi collisions. Turn on ligatures to correct these collisions, as seen in the third row.

HOW TO TURN ON LIGATURES

WORD 2003 & 2007 | *Neither supports automatic ligatures.*

WORD 2010 | *Supports ligatures in OpenType fonts only. Right-click in the text and select ‹Font› from the menu. Click the ‹Advanced› tab. Next to ‹Ligatures›, select ‹Standard Only› (or one of the more elaborate options).*

WORDPERFECT | *Does not support automatic ligatures.*

PAGES | *Inspector (command + option + i) ➜ document icon (first icon in the top row) ➜ ‹Document›. Near the bottom of the panel, check ‹Use ligatures›.*

"Why are you telling me about ligatures if word-processor support for them is so limited?" To their fans, ligatures are a hallmark of fine typesetting. You might turn out to be one of those people. I'm not, but I don't judge. If you're having a document professionally designed (e.g., BUSINESS CARDS or LETTERHEAD), you can specify ligatures—probably a good idea if you work at *Pfiffner & Piffle LLP*. Word processors are slowly improving, and in time, ligatures will be an option for more legal writers. But until then, ligatures are likely to remain on the typographic sidelines.

BY THE WAY

➜ Is it possible to insert ligatures manually? Yes. You can either insert them as you type from a character palette, or you can search and replace at the end. I don't recommend manually entering ligatures because they can confuse the spelling checker and the HYPHENATION engine, and end up causing more problems than they solve.

Specimen of fonts offered by William Caslon, 1728.

Text formatting

WHEN I TELL PEOPLE I WRITE ABOUT typography, they often say, "Oh, you mean fonts?"

Yes and no. Sure, fonts are an important part of typography. But there's much more to typography than fonts.

Similarly, there's more to text formatting than what font to use. Text formatting includes everything that affects the appearance of the characters on the page—not only fonts, but also point size, bold and italic styles, small caps, letterspacing, and kerning.

The first part of this chapter covers basic and advanced formatting rules. The second part is a gallery of font samples—for those ready to look beyond the limitations of SYSTEM FONTS.

In this chapter, there aren't as many bright lines between correct and incorrect habits as in the last chapter. You won't be able to get by on rote application of rules. You'll need to start making typographic judgments of your own.

Basic rules

In a printed document, don't underline. Ever. It's ugly and it makes text harder to read. See for yourself—

> Underlining is another holdover from the typewriter age. Typewriters had no bold or italic styling. So the only way to emphasize text was to back up the carriage and type underscores beneath the text. It was a workaround for shortcomings in typewriter technology.

Underlining is another holdover from the typewriter age. Typewriters had no bold or italic styling. So the only way to emphasize text was to back up the carriage and type underscores beneath the text. It was a workaround for shortcomings in typewriter technology.

Your word processor does not suffer from these shortcomings. If you feel the urge to underline, use BOLD OR ITALIC instead. In special situations, like HEADINGS, you can also consider using ALL CAPS, SMALL CAPS, or a change in POINT SIZE.

Not convinced? I invite you to find a book, newspaper, or magazine that underlines text. I notice it only in the tabloids. Is that the look you're going for? No, I didn't think so.

➡ Another reason underlining looks worse than bold or italic: underlining is mechanically applied by the word processor. Bold and italic styles are specially designed to match the basic style of the font.

➡ The "track changes" feature of your word processor will underline text added to the document. This is fine. In fact, it's one more reason *not* to use underlining for emphasis—to avoid confusing text marked as a revision with text that happens to be underlined.

➡ "But the *Bluebook* requires underlining." No, it doesn't. In its rules for practitioners, the *Bluebook* chooses to "keep[ ] with the tradition of underlining certain text," but practitioners "may substitute italic type wherever underlining is used." *Bluebook* at 3 (19th ed. 2010). Subsequent *Bluebook* rules say to "underscore (or italicize)." (For instance, *Bluebook* rule B1.) So unless you're using a typewriter, fulfill your *Bluebook* destiny by italicizing, not underlining.

➡ On a website, it's idiomatic to underline clickable text (also known as *hyperlinks*). But don't underline other text—visitors will be confused when their clicking goes unanswered.

I once met a lawyer who had actually set his letterhead in a font called Stencil:

goofy fonts
Don't use them

WILLARD N. KURTZ
ATTORNEY AT LAW

What was his target clientele? Army-surplus stores? He explained that he wanted something distinctive.

Distinctive is fine. Goofy is not.

Willard N. Kurtz

Willard N. Kurtz

Willard N. Kurtz

WILLARD N. KURTZ

WILLARD N. KURTZ

From the top: no, no, no, no, and hell no.

Novelty fonts, script fonts, handwriting fonts, circus fonts—these have no place in any document created by a lawyer. Save it for your next career as a designer of breakfast-cereal boxes.

monospaced fonts

Don't use these either

The SYSTEM FONTS Courier, Monaco, and Consolas are examples of *monospaced fonts*, so named because every character is the same width. Most other fonts are proportionally spaced, meaning the characters vary in width.

abcdefghijklmnopqrstuvwxyz!

abcdefghijklmnopqrstuvwxyz!

Jill, did you buy the milk?

Jill, did you buy the milk?

The samples above are set at the same POINT SIZE. But the monospaced font (first and third rows) takes up more horizontal space than the proportional font (second and fourth rows). The differences are most noticeable in characters that are narrow in the proportional font, like f, i, j, l, r, t, and the punctuation characters.

Monospaced fonts were invented to meet the mechanical requirements of typewriters. They were not invented to win beauty contests. Compared to proportional fonts, monospaced fonts are harder to read. And because they take up more horizontal space, you'll always get fewer words per page with a monospaced font.

There are no good reasons to use monospaced fonts. So don't. Use proportional fonts.

BY THE WAY

→ If you practice in one of the few courts that require a monospaced font, you can still do better than Courier. See FONT SAMPLES for better options, including FB Alix, a font family I designed to show that monospaced fonts for BODY TEXT don't have to be tedious.

→ Do you need monospaced numerals—typographers call them *tabular figures*—so that columns of numbers will line up? This is such a common need that most proportional fonts include tabular figures by default. To check if your font has them, type a line of zeroes above a line of ones. If they're the same length, the font has tabular figures.

00000000   00000000
11111111 TABULAR   11111111 NOT

→ Do you need to quote software code or HTML in your document? Then use a monospaced font for one of the reasons software engineers do—software code includes compressed syntax like (int i=1; i<111; i++) which is more legible when set in a monospaced font (int i=1; i<111; i++).

System fonts are the fonts already installed on your computer. Some are better than others. In printed documents they present three problems.

(1) *Many system fonts are not very good.* This is less of a problem on the Mac. But some of the Windows system fonts are among the most awful on the planet. I won't name names, but my least favorite rhymes with Barial.

(2) *Many system fonts have been optimized for screen legibility, not print.* This legibility comes at the cost of design details, which have been sanded off because they don't reproduce well on screen (e.g., Georgia, Verdana, Cambria, and Calibri). Screen-optimized fonts look clunky on the printed page.

In one square inch, an LCD screen that displays 100 dots per inch has less than 3% of the resolution of a laser printer with 600 dots per inch, so rendering a font accurately is much more difficult. It's analogous to the problem of scanning a paper document accurately—lower resolution means lower fidelity.

Rocket *Waxier* **Quad** GEORGIA
Rocket *Waxier* **Quad** MILLER

Compare the two fonts above. In basic appearance, they're similar. But Georgia was optimized for the screen; Miller was optimized for print. See the difference?

(3) *All system fonts are overexposed.* Because these fonts are included with millions of computers, they're used all the time. Not every typography project demands novelty, but if yours does, you'll need to look elsewhere. For instance, you wouldn't want to adopt the marketing slogan "A Law Firm Unlike Any Other" and then set it in Helvetica.

If you're limited to system fonts, consult this chart and choose wisely. For print, fonts on the A list are always best. For screen display, like presentations and websites, system fonts on the A, B, and C lists are fine. They're also suitable for sharing draft documents. But always steer clear of the F list.

The A list:
Generally tolerable
Baskerville (Mac) ★
Bell MT ★
Book Antiqua ★
Californian FB ★
Calisto MT ★
Century Schoolbook ★
Franklin Gothic ★
Garamond ★
Gill Sans ★
Gill Sans MT ★
Goudy Old Style ★
Helvetica ★
Helvetica Neue ★
Hoefler Text ★
Optima ★
Palatino ★

The B list:
OK in limited doses
Agency FB
Big Caslon
Bodoni MT
Calibri ★
Candara ★
Centaur
Century
Cochin
Constantia
Corbel
Didot
Eras Medium ITC
Futura ★
Geneva
Gloucester MT Extra Cond.
High Tower Text ★
Modern No. 20
Perpetua ★
Rockwell
Segoe UI ★
Tw Cen MT ★

The C list:
Questionable
Andale Mono
Baskerville Old Face
Berlin Sans FB
Bernard MT Condensed
Britannic Bold

Cambria ★
Castellar
Century Gothic
Consolas
Cooper Black
Copperplate
Copperplate Gothic
Courier
Courier New
Elephant
Engravers MT
Felix Titling
Footlight MT Light
Georgia
Goudy Stout
Haettenschweiler
Impact
Lucida (all styles)
Maiandra GD
Monaco
Niagara Solid & Engraved
Onyx
Plantagenet Cherokee
Poor Richard
Skia
Times New Roman ★
Wide Latin

The F list:
Fatal to your credibility
Algerian
American Typewriter
Apple Chancery
Arial (all styles)
Bauhaus 93
Blackadder ITC
Bradley Hand ITC
Broadway
Brush Script MT
Bookman Old Style
Chalkboard
Chiller
Colonna MT
Comic Sans MS
Curlz MT
Edwardian Script ITC
Forte
Freestyle Script
French Script MT
Gabriola

Gigi
Harlow Solid Italic
Harrington
Herculanum
Imprint MT Shadow
Informal Roman
Jokerman
Juice ITC
Kristen ITC
Kunstler Script
Magneto
Marker Felt
Matura MT Script Capitals
Mistral
Monotype Corsiva
OCR A Extended
Old English Text MT
Palace Script MT
Papyrus
Parchment
Playbill
Pristina
Rage Italic
Ravie
Script MT Bold
Snap ITC
Stencil
Showcard Gothic
Tahoma
Tempus Sans ITC
Trebuchet MS
Verdana
Viner Hand ITC
Vivaldi
Vladimir Script
Zapfino

Fonts plausible for
BODY TEXT are
marked with ★. Others
are usable for special
purposes (for instance,
LETTERHEAD).

This chart includes all the
common Windows and
Mac system fonts, plus
the Microsoft Office
fonts. System configu-
rations differ, so not
every font will be on
your computer. If you
don't see it in your font
menu, it's not installed.

These rankings represent
a blend of practical and
aesthetic considerations,
not absolute merit. Some
fonts on the F list aren't
bad, they're just inapt
for a law office. Similarly,
some fonts on the A list
are not my favorites, but
they're reasonably useful.

WARNING

This chart is offered
only as a harm-reduc-
tion device. In the long
term, a diet of system
fonts can be harmful
to your health. My of-
ficial advice remains
the same: lawyers are
professional writers,
and professional writ-
ers should use profes-
sional fonts. In FONT
SAMPLES, I suggest
professional fonts that
are good alternatives
to the most common
system fonts.

➡ "If my PDF will probably be read on screen, shouldn't I use a screen-optimized system font?" No. In Windows, fonts are optimized for the screen using *hinting*, which is extra software code stored in the font itself. Windows relies on this hinting when it draws text on screen (e.g., in Microsoft Word). But Adobe Acrobat—what most people use to read PDFs—draws text on screen using its own technology that ignores the hinting. So in PDF, system fonts lose their screen-legibility advantage over other fonts. Any PDF could also end up being printed. Therefore, as a rule, you're better off using print-optimized fonts for PDFs, regardless of how you expect the PDF to be read.

> Adobe uses its own text-rendering technology in Acrobat so that PDF documents display the same way on screen regardless of the underlying operating system.

➡ "But if I use a print-optimized professional font in my PDF instead of a system font, my readers probably won't have the same font installed." Right. But it doesn't matter. When you generate a PDF, your fonts are embedded in the PDF to preserve the formatting.

➡ My aversion to Comic Sans—king of the GOOFY FONTS—probably comes as no surprise. But why Arial? Arial was created as a Helvetica substitute. To many, they're indistinguishable.

Gothic **Fright** Refusal ARIAL
Gothic **Fright** Refusal HELVETICA

But to typographers, Arial contains none of the consistency and balance that makes Helvetica successful. For instance, the ends of the lowercase a, c, e, g, s, and t in Helvetica are exactly horizontal. In Arial, those ends are sloped arbitrarily. Reading Arial is like trying to have dinner on a tippy restaurant table.

As a system font, Arial has achieved ubiquity akin to TIMES NEW ROMAN. And like Times New Roman, Arial is permanently associated with the work of people who will never care about typography.

You're not one of those people. So use Helvetica. Use Franklin Gothic. Use Gill Sans. Use one of the other substitutes for Arial in FONT SAMPLES (see page 116). But don't use Arial.

Bold *or* italic—always think of them as mutually exclusive. That is the first rule.

The second rule is to use bold and italic as little as possible. They are tools for emphasis. But if everything is emphasized, then nothing is emphasized. Also, because bold and italic styles are designed to contrast with regular roman text, they're somewhat harder to read. They're fine for short pieces of text, but not for long stretches.

Nevertheless, some lawyers—let's call them *overemphasizers*—just can't get enough bold and italic. If they feel strongly about the point they're making, they won't hesitate to run the whole paragraph in bold type. Don't be one of these people. This habit wears down your readers' retinas and their patience. It also gives you nowhere to go when you need to emphasize a word. That's no problem for overemphasizers, who resort to <u>underlining bold text</u> or *using bold italic*. <u>*These are both bad ideas.*</u>

With a serif font, use italic for gentle emphasis, or bold for heavier emphasis.

Please *emphasize* this RIGHT

Please **emphasize** this RIGHT

If you're using a sans serif font, skip italic and use bold for emphasis. It's usually not worth italicizing sans serif fonts—unlike serif fonts, which look quite different when italicized, most sans serif italic fonts just have a gentle slant that doesn't stand out on the page.

Please *emphasize* this WRONG

Please **emphasize** this RIGHT

Text that is neither bold nor italic is called **roman**.

Serif fonts like Georgia and Palatino have "feet" protruding from the ends of vertical strokes. These feet are the serifs. Serif rhymes with **sheriff**, not **sir reef**.

Sans serif fonts like Helvetica and Verdana do not have these feet. Though they are associated with contemporary typography, sans serif fonts date from the 1810s. Sans rhymes with **hands**, not **cons**. Avoid the common misspelling **san serif**.

→ Foreign words used in English are sometimes italicized, sometimes not, depending on how common they are. For instance, you would italicize your *bête noire* and your *Weltanschauung*, but not your croissant or your résumé. When in doubt, consult a dictionary or usage guide.

→ One reason I don't recommend sans serif fonts for BODY TEXT is because they have weak italic styles. Legal citations are more legible with a distinct italic.

→ See HEADINGS for tips on how to avoid escalating overemphasis when working with multiple heading levels.

→ If you need another option for emphasis, consider SMALL CAPS.

→ Some fonts have both a bold style and a semibold style. You can use either for emphasis. I usually prefer bold to semibold because I like the greater contrast. But semibold is a little easier to read.

→ Some fonts have styles that are heavier than bold, like black or ultra. These weights are usually intended for large sizes (for instance, headlines) and don't work well at the 10- to 12-point range of most BODY TEXT.

all caps

Fine for less than one line

All-caps text—meaning text with all the letters capitalized—is best used sparingly.

At standard BODY TEXT sizes, capital letters—or simply *caps*—are harder to read than normal lowercase text. Why? We read more lowercase text, so as a matter of habit, lowercase is more familiar and thus more legible. Furthermore, cognitive research has suggested that the shapes of lowercase letters—some tall (dhkl), some short (aens), some descending (gypq)—create a varied visual contour that helps our brain recognize words. Capitalization homogenizes these shapes, leaving a rectangular contour.

Legible Shapes
LEGIBLE SHAPES

VARIED

RECTANGULAR

That doesn't mean you shouldn't use caps. Just use them judiciously. Caps are suitable for headings shorter than one line (e.g., "TABLE OF AUTHORITIES"), headers, footers, captions, or other labels. Caps work at small POINT SIZES. Caps work well on LETTERHEAD and BUSINESS CARDS. Always add LETTERSPACING to caps to make them easier to read, and make sure KERNING is turned on.

DON'T CAPITALIZE WHOLE PARAGRAPHS. THIS HABIT IS ENDEMIC TO LAWYERS, BUT IT'S ESPECIALLY COMMON IN CONTRACTS. MANY LAWYERS SEEM TO THINK THAT CAPITALIZATION COMMUNICATES AUTHORITY AND IMPORTANCE. "HEY, LOOK HERE, I'M A LAWYER! I DEMAND THAT YOU PAY ATTENTION TO THIS!" BUT A PARAGRAPH SET IN ALL CAPS IS VERY HARD TO READ. **AND IT'S EVEN HARDER TO READ IF IT'S BOLD. AS THE PARAGRAPH WEARS ON, READERS FATIGUE. INTEREST WANES. HOW ABOUT YOU? DO YOU ENJOY READING THIS? I DOUBT IT. BUT I REGULARLY SEE CAPITALIZED PARAGRAPHS IN LEGAL DOCUMENTS THAT ARE MUCH LONGER THAN THIS. DO YOUR READERS A FAVOR. STOP CAPITALIZING WHOLE PARAGRAPHS.**

All-caps paragraphs are an example of self-defeating typography. If you need readers to pay attention to an important part of your document, the last thing you want is for them to skim over it. But that's what inevitably happens with all-caps paragraphs, because they're so difficult to read.

The terms **uppercase** and **lowercase** come from traditional print shops. Capital letters, used less frequently, were stored in a case on a shelf above the other letters (then called **minuscule** letters).

To emphasize a paragraph, you have better options. Use RULES AND BORDERS. Add a HEADING that labels it **Important**. Run it in a larger POINT SIZE. But don't capitalize it.

There are two ways to put caps in a document. The popular method is to engage the caps-lock key at the left edge of the keyboard and type away. That works, but it makes capitalization a permanent feature of your text.

The preferred method is to apply all-caps formatting to normally typed text. That way, you can toggle capitalization on and off without retyping the text itself.

	WORD	WORDPERFECT	PAGES
all caps	*control +* *shift + a*	*control + k* *(converts case)*	‹Format› ➙ ‹Font› ➙ ‹Capitalization› ➙ ‹All Caps›

BY THE WAY

➙ It can be useful to capitalize specially defined terms to distinguish them from their generic counterparts. But capitalize only the first letter. Don't set the whole word in caps, or worse, bold caps. Likewise, you can refer to party Omicron Motor Company as Omicron—you don't need to write its name OMICRON or **OMICRON**. When you set a word like **OMICRON** in caps, you're putting a visual speed bump in every sentence that mentions **OMICRON**. As the habit multiplies, soon you're talking about how **OMICRON** and **SIGMA** conspired to make **AIRBAGS** that injured the **PLAINTIFF** and the rest of the **CLASS**. At that point, you haven't made your **DOCUMENT** easier to **READ**. You've only **MADE** it more **ANNOYING**.

➙ Sometimes caps are required by law—for instance, California requires that defined terms in discovery requests be set in all caps. (E.g., Cal. Civ. Proc. Code § 2030.060(e).) And sometimes caps are prohibited by law—for instance, New York court rules say that "[e]xcept in headings, words shall not be in bold type or type consisting of all capital letters." (22 N.Y.C.R.R. 500.1(j).)

➤ Don't assume caps are either necessary or sufficient to satisfy a law requiring "conspicuous" text. For instance, the Uniform Commercial Code defines "conspicuous" as "written, displayed, or presented [so] that a reasonable person against which it is to operate ought to have noticed it," but notes that "[w]hether a term is 'conspicuous' or not is a decision for the court." (UCC § 1-201(b)(10).) The Ninth Circuit has held that "[l]awyers who think their caps lock keys are instant 'make conspicuous' buttons are deluded. In determining whether a term is conspicuous, we look at more than formatting." (*In re Bassett*, 285 F.3d 882, 886 (9th Cir. 2002).) So should you.

➤ If your all-caps text contains a citation with a small-letter subdivision, don't capitalize the subdivision letter—it may render the citation ambiguous or incorrect.

CIV. CODE § 1744(A)   WRONG
CIV. CODE § 1744(a)   RIGHT

➤ "Why reject UNDERLINING but not caps? Aren't they both typewriter habits?" No. Caps are the original alphabetic characters. They are part of the oldest traditions of our written language. Underlining cannot claim a similar pedigree. Caps in English descend directly from the Latin alphabet. (That's why basic, unstyled fonts are called *roman.*) Through the early Middle Ages, scribes in Europe adapted the Latin alphabet into smaller, more casual forms, called *minuscules.* In the 700s, Charlemagne started a project to create a standardized script across his empire. That script, *Carolingian minuscule,* spread through Europe and popularized the combination of uppercase and lowercase letters that's been a feature of printed European languages since then.

➤ To those lawyers who type e-mails in all caps: enough already. YOU DON'T HAVE TO SHOUT. WE CAN HEAR YOU JUST FINE.

point size

Smaller on paper; bigger on screen

There are 72 **points** to an inch. Word lets you specify point sizes in half-point increments. WordPerfect and Pages allow finer increments of one-tenth of a point.

The *point size* of your text can be smaller than you think. The optimal point size for BODY TEXT in printed documents is between 10 and 12 point.

While courts often require text to be set at 12 point—and sometimes larger—it's not the most comfortable size for reading. If you compare a court filing with the average book, newspaper, or magazine, you'll notice that the text in the filing is larger.

When you're not bound by court rules, don't treat 12 point as the minimum. Try sizes down to 10 point, including intermediate sizes like 10.5 and 11.5 point—half-point differences are meaningful at this scale. (This paragraph is set at 11 point.)

When you're not bound by court rules, don't treat 12 point as the minimum. Try sizes down to 10 point, including intermediate sizes like 10.5 and 11.5 point—half-point differences are meaningful at this scale. (This paragraph is set at 10.5 point.)

When you're not bound by court rules, don't treat 12 point as the minimum. Try sizes down to 10 point, including intermediate sizes like 10.5 and 11.5 point—half-point differences are meaningful at this scale. (This paragraph is set at 10 point.)

This paragraph is set at 12 point. The text looks oversized compared to the other paragraphs, doesn't it? It's very difficult to find a professionally designed book, newspaper, or magazine with 12-point body text. One major reason is cost—bigger point sizes require more paper.

But I can't guarantee 12 point will always look too big. That's because the point-size system is not absolute—different fonts set at the same point size won't necessarily appear the same on the page.

That means you need to let your eyes be the judge. Don't just rely on the point size. For instance, the three fonts below—Sabon, TIMES NEW ROMAN, and Arno—are set at 12 point, but they're not the same size visually.

Different fonts set at the same point size won't necessarily appear the same size on the page. Let your eyes be the judge. Don't just rely on the point size.	SABON 12 POINT
Different fonts set at the same point size won't necessarily appear the same size on the page. Let your eyes be the judge. Don't just rely on the point size.	TIMES NEW ROMAN 12 POINT
Different fonts set at the same point size won't necessarily appear the same size on the page. Let your eyes be the judge. Don't just rely on the point size.	ARNO 12 POINT

You can match the length of two fonts by setting a block of text twice: once in the old font and once in the new font, both at the same point size. Adjust the point size of the new font until each line of text breaks in roughly the same place. (You won't be able to match them exactly.) Below, the point sizes of Sabon and Arno have been adjusted so they occupy the same space as Times New Roman.

Different fonts set at the same point size won't necessarily appear the same size on the page. Let your eyes be the judge. Don't just rely on the point size.	SABON 11 POINT
Different fonts set at the same point size won't necessarily appear the same size on the page. Let your eyes be the judge. Don't just rely on the point size.	TIMES NEW ROMAN 12 POINT
Different fonts set at the same point size won't necessarily appear the same size on the page. Let your eyes be the judge. Don't just rely on the point size.	ARNO 13 POINT

The point size can be even smaller in professionally typeset materials like publications and stationery. Text on BUSINESS CARDS is often only seven or eight points. ALL CAPS text is often just as legible as regular lowercase text at these sizes.

For websites, I recommend 12 point or larger for body text. On screen, even 13 or 14 point can be a comfortable reading size. The web has a tradition of teeny fonts—web designers have long insisted on accommodating some hypothetical guy in Sioux Falls who's still using a Windows 95 machine, a 13-inch monitor, and a 2400-baud modem. I feel comfortable ignoring him.

POINT SIZE AS EMPHASIS

It's fine to emphasize text with a larger point size (or de-emphasize it with a smaller point size). If you use BOLD OR ITALIC, or ALL CAPS, the styling is binary: it's either **ON** or off. But point size offers a subtle range of adjustments.

You can also emphasize text by applying bold or all-caps formatting, and then **reducing** the point size slightly. Sounds strange but it can work.

The key word: *subtle*. If the text is set at 11 point, you don't need to go up to 14 point for emphasis. Start with a small increase—say, half a point—and move up in half-point increments until you get the emphasis you need.

BY THE WAY

➡ In a legal document, I can't imagine any reason to use a font smaller than seven point or larger than 30 point.

➡ In HYPHENS AND DASHES, I mentioned that *em* refers to a typographer's measurement, not the letter M. The em size of a font is the same as its point size. Digital fonts are made of scalable outlines, not metal, but the em terminology persists. Digital fonts are drawn inside a rectangle called the em. To render a font on screen, your computer scales the em to match the current point size. Two fonts set at the same point size will appear to be different sizes if one occupies less space on its em.

➤ As you reduce point size, also reduce LINE SPACING and LINE LENGTH. For instance, newspaper fonts are quite small, but remain legible because they have snug line spacing and short line length.

➤ Most courts control the length of briefs with limits on point size and page length. In the typewriter age, this worked because typewriter output was standardized. In the digital age, it makes less sense, since artful formatting and layout can make documents appear longer or shorter as necessary. (If you're unclear on the concept, ask someone who's written a college paper in the last 20 years.) Courts, law professors, and anyone else who needs to set standards for document length would be better off putting these rules in terms of word count. Unlike typewriters, all word processors have a word-count function. Compared to page limits, word counts are harder to evade. To be fair, they're also harder to verify.

➤ Can you determine the point size of a font by measuring it? No. Because of the differences in apparent sizing between fonts, there's nothing you can measure that would be conclusive. The only way to figure it out is to set the same text, in the same font, with the same LINE LENGTH. Then adjust the point size so it matches the printed sample.

➤ If lawyers have established a reputation for anything typographic, it is our legendary affection for *fine print*. Fine print is synonymous with evasion and deception. I have some trepidation about advising that "the point size of your text can be smaller than you think" because I don't want to encourage the fine-print abusers out there. You know who you are. ("Did you hear that? Butterick said we can crank it down *even smaller!*")

Good typography reinforces the goals of the text (as you may remember from WHAT IS GOOD TYPOGRAPHY). Lawyers are advocates, so when I dispense typographic advice, I'm careful not to take a position on the propriety of certain habits.

For instance, as a consumer, I don't like getting a credit-card contract that's an acre of six-point type. But if I were a lawyer for the credit-card company, my job would be to advance the interests of my client, including the typography.

If that seems cruelly pragmatic, consider direct-mail solicitations. I find them ugly and unappealing. But I also know their design is the result of years of testing and refinement about how to get people to part with their money. Is that good typography? In context, yes.

"Did you hear that? Butterick said that fine print can be *good typography!*" Touché, I guess.

Advanced rules

Headings present two sets of problems for lawyers: structural and typographic. Cure the structural problems and the typographic problems become much simpler.

The first structural problem is that lawyers often use too many levels of headings. This leads to increasingly desperate attempts to make them visually distinct, usually with injudicious combinations of BOLD OR ITALIC, UNDERLINING, POINT SIZE, ALL CAPS, and FIRST-LINE INDENTS. The result is pileups like this:

> ***<u>iv.) The Defendant Has Sufficient Minimum Contacts with California.</u>***

Headings are signposts for readers that reveal the structure of your argument. Note that I didn't say the structure of your *document*. Headings that announce every topic, subtopic, minitopic, and microtopic are exhausting. If you write from an outline, that can be a good starting point for your headings, but don't stop there—simplify it further.

Limit yourself to three levels of headings. Two is better. Readers should be able to orient themselves from the headings. With more than three levels, that task becomes hopelessly confusing. You may know your argument inside out, but no one else does.

The second structural problem is headings that are just placeholders or labels. Write substantive headings. Readers should be able to understand the framework of your argument just by reading the headings. Headings without substance are not signposts—they just waste space. Here's a bad heading:

I.   **INTRODUCTION**

In journalism, **burying the lead** describes the error of putting the key idea of your story somewhere in the middle. Traditionally it was spelled **lede**, not **lead**, to distinguish it from the material used for casting metal type.

Whatever appears under the first heading is obviously the introduction. So avoid a generic label and make the heading descriptive. Is your introduction framing the legal issue? Summarizing the procedural history? Reciting facts? Then say so:

I.   **Legal issue**

I.   **Procedural history**

I.   **Facts**

Another bad heading:

B.   **For the reasons below, the Court should find that it has personal jurisdiction over the defendant.**

This heading isn't a signpost—it's a roadblock. Headings preview what's ahead. So move the argument forward. An improvement:

B.   **The Court has personal jurisdiction over MegaCorp because its headquarters are in San Luis Obispo.**

Once you've cured the structural problems, the typographic problems are easy to solve. If you simplify your headings, you'll end up needing only two or three levels. Then work within these parameters:

① Don't use ALL CAPS. If your headings are full sentences, they're too long for caps.

② Don't underline. Why? Review UNDERLINING.

③ Don't center, subject to the exceptions in CENTERED TEXT.

④ Use bold, not italic. For headings, bold is easier to read than italic and stands out better on the page. And since the choice is BOLD OR ITALIC—not both—you should prefer bold. (But it's still an option, not a requirement. Non-bold headings work too.)

⑤ It's fine to make the POINT SIZE bigger, but just a little. Use the smallest increment necessary to make a visible difference. If your text is set in 12 point, you needn't go up to 14 or 15 point. Try a smaller increase—to 12.5 or 13 point.

> If you're using bold in your heading, you can also try reducing the point size by a half or full point. If your font has a relatively heavy bold style (like TIMES NEW ROMAN), reducing the size slightly can offset the effect of the darker color, giving you subtler emphasis.

⑥ Only use two levels of indenting, even if you use more than two levels of headings. Some lawyers like to indent every heading a little farther. Bad idea. Once your heading is no longer anchored to something on the left edge of the text, it's just floating in space.

⑦ Suppress HYPHENATION in headings.

⑧ Use the KEEP LINES TOGETHER and KEEP WITH NEXT PARAGRAPH options to prevent headings from breaking awkwardly across pages.

See HIERARCHICAL HEADINGS for tips on how to number headings.

Kerning is the adjustment of specific pairs of letters to improve spacing and fit. (It differs from LETTERSPACING, which affects all pairs.) Most fonts come with hundreds and sometimes thousands of kerning pairs inserted by the font designer.

Below, notice how kerning reduces the large gaps between certain letter pairs, making them consistent with the rest of the font.

"AY, Ty, Va, TAT."   KERNING OFF

"AY, Ty, Va, TAT."   KERNING ON

Always use kerning. By default, kerning is not activated in Word or WordPerfect, so you have to turn it on yourself. If you use PARAGRAPH AND CHARACTER STYLES, turn on kerning as part of your style definitions.

HOW TO TURN ON KERNING

WORD | *Right-click in the text and select ‹Font› from the menu. Click the ‹Character Spacing› tab. (In Word 2010 it's called the ‹Advanced› tab.) Check the box that says ‹Kerning for fonts _____ Points and above›. Put the number 8 in the point-size box.*

WORDPERFECT | ‹Format› → ‹Typesetting› → ‹Word/Letter Spacing› → ‹Automatic Kerning›

PAGES | *Kerning is on by default and cannot be turned off.*

kerning

Turn it on

It's also possible to manually kern letter pairs. For professional typographers, this is a mandatory skill, but for everyone else, the built-in kerning is adequate.

letterspacing

Use 5–12% extra space with caps, but not with lowercase

Letterspacing (also known as *character spacing* or *tracking*) is the adjustment of the horizontal white space between the letters in a block of text. Unlike KERNING, which affects only designated pairs of letters, letterspacing affects every pair.

PALACE   THIEF   NO LETTERSPACING

PALACE   THIEF   LETTERSPACED

Lowercase letters don't ordinarily need letterspacing. Capital letters usually appear at the beginning of a word or sentence, so they're designed to fit correctly next to lowercase letters. But when you use capital letters together, that spacing is too tight.

That's why you always add 5–12% extra letterspacing to text in ALL CAPS or SMALL CAPS. This is particularly important at small sizes (e.g., the footer of a court filing).

HOW TO SET LETTERSPACING

WORD | *Right-click in the text and select ‹Font› from the menu. Click the ‹Character Spacing› tab. (In Word 2010 it's called the ‹Advanced› tab.) On the line that says ‹Spacing›, in the box on the right, enter the amount of letterspacing. Letterspacing in Word is measured in points. Use 0.6–1.4 points of letterspacing for every 12 points of point size (this corresponds to 5–12%).*

WORDPERFECT | *‹Format› ➜ ‹Typesetting› ➜ ‹Word/Letter Spacing›. In the box labeled ‹Letterspacing: Percent of Optimal›, enter the amount of letterspacing. Letterspacing in WordPerfect is measured as a percentage of normal spacing. Use 105–112%.*

PAGES | *Inspector (command + option + i) ➜ T icon in the top row (fourth from left). Use the ‹Character› slider to add letterspacing. Letterspacing in Pages is measured as percent added. Use 5–12%.*

These are not absolute limits—use your judgment. But avoid the common error of spreading letters too far apart. If the spaces between letters are large enough to fit more letters, you've gone overboard.

T O U L O U S E   WRONG

PAS TOULOUSE   RIGHT

BY THE WAY

➡ Typographer Frederic Goudy is famously credited with opining that "Anyone who would letterspace lowercase would steal sheep." But a few sources claim that his original comment concerned blackletter fonts, not lowercase, and that he used a more colorful verb than "steal."

➡ I accept the minority view on Goudy's comment because, as Goudy was doubtless aware, sometimes lowercase should be letterspaced. Fonts intended for BODY TEXT have spacing optimized for body-text point sizes (approximately 9–13 point). But typographers will often add letterspacing to lowercase text smaller than nine point in order to keep the spaces between letters distinct. Similarly, typographers will often remove letterspacing from lowercase text used at larger sizes (e.g., headlines).

➡ As with KERNING, if you use PARAGRAPH AND CHARACTER STYLES to make a style with all caps or small caps, include letterspacing as part of the style definition.

ein

blackletter font

The sidebars in this book are set at 8.5 point, so I've added a small amount of extra letterspacing, as seen in this paragraph.

But in this paragraph, I've restored the normal letterspacing. It's a subtle difference, but a touch of extra letter-spacing keeps small text from looking congested.

color

Black is best

Color used to be irrelevant to a law office that only had access to monochrome printers and copiers. These days, color output devices are cheap and ubiquitous, so the topic deserves a brief mention.

Printed documents intended for reading (e.g., MOTIONS, RE-SEARCH MEMOS, letters) should always be set in black type. No exceptions.

Some documents (e.g., LETTERHEAD, BUSINESS CARDS) can include text set in color, but use it judiciously. Multiple shades of one color are usually better than multiple contrasting colors.

In printed documents, avoid white text on a dark background, known as *knockout* text. Knockout text uses about 20 times more toner than regular text, making it a very expensive effect on an office laser printer.

BY THE WAY

➡ On websites, consider making your text dark gray rather than black. Unlike a piece of paper—which reflects ambient light—a computer's LCD screen projects its own light and tends to have more severe contrast. Therefore, on screen, dark gray text is often more comfortable to read than black text. That's why many digital-book readers let you reduce the screen brightness or change the text color.

➡ I recommend color for digital BATES NUMBERING because it's meant to stand out on the page.

➡ I don't like to use gray backgrounds in documents intended for laser printing. The original might look fine, but subsequent copying or scanning tends to make the gray backgrounds darker and grittier, making the text less legible.

ordinals

No superscripts

Ordinals are numbers that express position in a series. By default, your word processor will convert ordinals into superscripts.

1st	2nd	304th	SUPERSCRIPTS
1st	2nd	304th	NO SUPERSCRIPTS

Superscripted ordinals have two problems. First, ordinals turn up most often in citations. The *Bluebook* and other citation authorities forbid superscripted ordinals (e.g., *Bluebook* rule 6.2(b)(i) (19th ed. 2010)). Second, superscripted ordinals are tiny and hard to read.

The best practice is to avoid superscripted ordinals. To do this, you have to adjust your word processor's default behavior.

HOW TO TURN OFF SUPERSCRIPTED ORDINALS

WORD 2003 | ‹Tools› → ‹AutoCorrect Options› → ‹AutoFormat As You Type› → *uncheck* ‹Ordinals (1st) with superscript›

WORD 2007 | *Office menu* → ‹Word Options› → ‹Proofing› → ‹AutoCorrect Options› → ‹AutoFormat As You Type› → *uncheck* ‹Ordinals (1st) with superscript›

WORD 2010 | ‹File› → ‹Options› → ‹Proofing› → ‹AutoCorrect Options› → ‹AutoFormat As You Type› → *uncheck* ‹Ordinals (1st) with superscript›

WORDPERFECT | ‹Tools› → ‹QuickCorrect› → ‹Format-As-You-Go› → *uncheck* ‹QuickOrdinals› *(under* ‹Format-As-You-Go Choices›*)*

PAGES | ‹Pages› → ‹Preferences› → ‹Auto-Correction› → *uncheck* ‹Superscript numerical suffixes›

web & e-mail addresses

Don't hyphenate

Web addresses identify a location on the Internet. They usually take the form http://www.somelongname.com/folder/folder/page.html. *E-mail addresses* usually take the form nameofperson@somelongname.com.

Web addresses present two problems.

The first problem: web addresses can be long. Really, really long. Running the whole web address may be fine if you're writing a law-review footnote and just need to show where you got your material. But it's useless if you're hoping readers will type the address on their own.

URL stands for **Uniform Resource Locator**. It's another name for a web address.

For a more usable web address, use an address-shortening service like TinyURL or Bit.ly. These services take a web address of any length and convert it into a short address like http://tinyurl.com/p5wf3c. This is easier to read and type. But it doesn't reveal the underlying web address. It also isn't guaranteed to work permanently.

If you put a web address in a citation, consider running the long version with a shortened version next to it. Then you're covered. For instance:

> *See* http://www.cacd.uscourts.gov/CACD/LocRules.nsf/a224d2a6f8771599882567cc005e9d79/043e35b5803a6d3f8825768d0067b375?OpenDocument, *also available at* http://tinyurl.com/y6o4yte.

The second problem: web addresses are difficult to wrap onto multiple lines. A web address is one unbroken string of characters. You don't want your web address hyphenated, because readers will likely mistake the hyphens for part of the address. Therefore, use HARD LINE BREAKS to set the points where the web address should wrap onto the next line.

E-mail addresses are shorter than web addresses and aren't as painful to work with. But they shouldn't be hyphenated either, for the same reasons.

Word processors have an annoying default habit of making every web and e-mail address underlined and blue. That might make some sense if you're creating a PDF that needs to include hyperlinks. But it makes no sense at all if you're creating a document that needs to be printed.

HOW TO TURN OFF AUTOMATIC HYPERLINKS

WORD 2003 | ‹Tools› ➡ ‹AutoCorrect Options› ➡ ‹AutoFormat As You Type› ➡ *uncheck* ‹Internet and network paths with hyperlinks›

WORD 2007 | *Office menu* ➡ ‹Word Options› ➡ ‹Proofing› ➡ ‹AutoCorrect Options› ➡ ‹AutoFormat As You Type› ➡ *uncheck* ‹Internet and network paths with hyperlinks›

WORD 2010 | ‹File› ➡ ‹Options› ➡ ‹Proofing› ➡ ‹AutoCorrect Options› ➡ ‹AutoFormat As You Type› ➡ *uncheck* ‹Internet and network paths with hyperlinks›

WORDPERFECT | ‹Tools› ➡ ‹QuickCorrect› ➡ ‹SpeedLinks› ➡ *uncheck* ‹Format words as hyperlinks when you type them›

PAGES | ‹Pages› ➡ ‹Preferences› ➡ ‹Auto-Correction› ➡ *uncheck* ‹Automatically detect e-mail and web addresses›

BY THE WAY

➡ What about typography within e-mails? Your options are limited. Unlike a PDF, fonts don't get transmitted with an e-mail. So even though you can compose an e-mail in any font you like, recipients won't see that font unless they also happen to have it installed. Moreover, recipients read e-mail on a variety of devices, which have different and unpredictable typographic capabilities. My policy: treat e-mail as a typography-free zone.

Use real small caps; avoid fakes

Small caps are short capital letters designed to blend with lowercase text. They're usually slightly taller than lowercase letters. (Small caps are used in this book to denote CROSS-REFERENCES.)

I'm a big fan of small caps. They look great and they're very useful as an alternative to BOLD OR ITALIC or ALL CAPS.

But most people have never seen real small caps. They've only seen the ersatz small caps that word processors generate when small-cap formatting is used.

WITNESS PROTECTION   FAKE

WITNESS PROTECTION   REAL

Trixie Argon, *Ways to Be Wicked*, in
CONJURING LITIGATION 2004, at 137–39
(London, Quid Pro Books, 2004).   FAKE

Trixie Argon, *Ways to Be Wicked*, in
CONJURING LITIGATION 2004, at 137–39
(London, Quid Pro Books, 2004).   REAL

Small-cap formatting works by scaling down regular caps. But compared to the other characters in the font, the fake small caps that result are too tall, and their vertical strokes are too light. The color and height of real small caps have been calibrated to blend well with the normal uppercase and lowercase letters.

Typographers use the word **color** to refer to how light or dark a text block appears on a page (even if all the characters are black).

Therefore, two rules for small caps:

(1) Don't click on the small-cap formatting box in your word processor. Ever. This option does not produce small caps. It produces inferior counterfeits.

②　The rules for ALL CAPS also apply to small caps: use small caps sparingly, add LETTERSPACING, and turn on KERNING.

Now for the bad news. If you want real small caps, you'll have to buy them—they're not included with TIMES NEW ROMAN or any other SYSTEM FONT.

Usually, small caps come in their own font file that shows up separately in the font menu. When you want small caps, you format the text with the small-cap font. You can also use PARAGRAPH AND CHARACTER STYLES to apply small caps, and eliminate most of the tedium of using a separate font.

BY THE WAY

➤　With small caps, it's up to you whether to use regular capital letters at the beginning of capitalized words. For instance, a footer could read FIRST AMENDED COMPLAINT or FIRST AMENDED COMPLAINT. I prefer the latter.

➤　Even if you get a small-cap font, the small-cap formatting box will still give you fake small caps. To avoid confusion, just forget the formatting box exists.

➤　Many new fonts are sold in the OpenType format instead of the older TrueType format. Font designers prefer OpenType because it allows small caps to be built into the main font. Unfortunately, word-processor support for this feature is weak. Neither Word nor WordPerfect supports OpenType small caps. (Pages does.) So most lawyers will be stuck with the traditional technique of using a separate small-cap font. If you buy a professional font family (like the ones shown in FONT SAMPLES), be sure to find out if you can get the small caps in a separate TrueType file.

➤　"Can I get real small caps that match TIMES NEW ROMAN?" Yes you can. Monotype Imaging, the company that owns Times New Roman, also sells the accompanying small caps. Enter code 11801 on the Typography for Lawyers website.

hierarchical headings

Consider tiered numbers

Traditionally, *hierarchical headings* in legal documents start with roman numerals at the top level (I, II, III); then switch to capital letters (A, B, C); then to arabic numerals (1, 2, 3); then to lowercase letters (a, b, c); then to romanettes (i, ii, iii); then to variations of the above using two parentheses instead of one, or other barely visible changes.

This is a terrible way to label hierarchical headings.

Yes, that's what they're called—**romanettes**.

① Roman numerals and romanettes stink. They're difficult to read. (Quick, what number is XLIX?) They're easy to confuse at a glance. (II vs. III, IV vs. VI, XXI vs. XII.) If what we mean by I, II, III is 1, 2, 3, then let's just say so.

② Letters are not much better because while we immediately recognize A, B, C as equivalent to 1, 2, 3, the letter-to-number correlation gets weaker as we go past F, G, H. (Quick, what number is T?) If what we mean by J, K, L is 10, 11, 12, then let's just say so.

③ Mixing roman numerals and letters results in ambiguous references—when you see a lowercase *i*, does it denote the first item or the ninth item? Does a lowercase *v* denote the fifth item or the 22nd item?

④ By using only one index on each header, it's easy to lose track of where you are in the hierarchy. If I'm at subheading *d*, is that *d* under superheading 2 or 3?

Lawyers should take a cue from technical writers, who solved this problem long ago—by using tiered numbers as indexes for hierarchical headings.

So instead of:

I.   Primary heading
    A.   Secondary heading
    B.   Another secondary heading
        1.   Tertiary heading
        2.   Another tertiary heading
    C.   Another secondary heading
II.   Another primary heading

You'd have:

1.   Primary heading
    1.1   Secondary heading
    1.2   Another secondary heading
        1.2.1   Tertiary heading
        1.2.2   Another tertiary heading
    1.3   Another secondary heading
2.   Another primary heading

To my eyes, this system is more understandable, because it only uses numbers. It's also more navigable, because it's always clear from a tiered number where you are in the hierarchy. And every modern word processor can automatically produce tiered numbers. Consider it.

mixing fonts

Less is more

Enthusiasm for fonts often leads to enthusiasm for multiple fonts, and then the question: "How do I get better at *mixing fonts* in a document?"

Mixing fonts is like mixing patterned shirts and ties—there aren't blackletter rules. Some people have a knack for it; some don't.

For instance: I recently had to attend a two-day lecture. I prefer not to dignify the speaker's presentation software by mentioning its name. Suffice it to say that her slides were both powerless and pointless.

But the slides did run through just about every SYSTEM FONT, and often multiple fonts per slide. I passed the time by inventing a system-font drinking game.

That story is offered as a caution, not a deterrent. I encourage you to try mixing fonts. It's a useful skill. Learning it will help you develop your eye for typography.

Bear in mind these general principles.

(1) Mixing fonts is never a requirement—it's an option. You can get plenty of mileage out of one font using variations based on POINT SIZE, BOLD OR ITALIC, SMALL CAPS, and so on.

(2) The rule of diminishing returns applies. Most documents can tolerate a second font; many fewer can tolerate a third; almost none can tolerate four or more. (If you're making a presentation, treat all the slides as one document.)

See the sidebar on page 85 for the difference between serif and sans serif fonts.

(3) You can mix any two fonts that are identifiably different. If you've heard you can only mix a serif font with a sans serif font, it's not true. Much like mixing colors, lower contrast between fonts can be more effective than higher contrast.

For instance, you would never mix Palatino and Palatino Nova (page 119)—the differences are too subtle. But I could easily see mixing Lyon and Harriet (page 121), even though they're both serif fonts. (And I do so throughout this book, at the beginning of each chapter.) You can also look at any American newspaper—typically, the BODY TEXT and the headlines are both in serif fonts, but different ones.

④ Font mixing is most successful when each font has a consistent role in the document. In a RESEARCH MEMO, try one font for body text and one font for HEADINGS. Or in a MOTION, try one font for things in the center of the document (body text and headings) and one font for things at the edges (line numbers, footer, and other miscellany). Or in BULLETED AND NUMBERED LISTS, try one font for the bullet or number and one font for the text of the list item—a technique I use throughout this book.

⑤ It rarely works to have multiple fonts in a single paragraph. Better to restrict yourself to one font per paragraph, and change fonts only at paragraph breaks.

⑥ While I'm reluctant to endorse rote methods, this one works pretty reliably: mix fonts by the same font designer. For instance, Palatino Nova (page 119) and Optima Nova (page 128), both the work of font designer Hermann Zapf, would mix well.

A BRIEF HISTORY OF
TIMES NEW ROMAN

Times New Roman gets its name from the *Times* of London, the British newspaper. In 1929, the *Times* hired typographer Stanley Morison of Monotype, a British font foundry, to create a new text font. Morison led the project and supervised Victor Lardent, an advertising artist for the *Times*, who drew the letterforms.

After Monotype completed Times New Roman, it had to license the design to then-rival Linotype, because the *Times* used Linotype's typesetting machines. (Think of Monotype and Linotype as the Depression-era Microsoft and Apple.) Since then, Monotype has sold the font as "Times New Roman" and Linotype has marketed its version as "Times Roman."

Typesetting technology has evolved since then, but due to its enduring popularity, Times New Roman has always been one of the first fonts available in each new format. This, in turn, has only increased its reach.

In 1984, Apple licensed Times Roman for the Macintosh; in 1992, Microsoft licensed Times New Roman for Windows. This put the font into the hands of millions of new users. The number of documents set in Times New Roman exploded.

Objectively, there's nothing wrong with Times New Roman. It was designed for a newspaper, so it's a bit narrower than most text fonts—**especially the bold style**. (Newspapers prefer narrow fonts because they fit more text per line.) *The italic is mediocre.* But those aren't fatal flaws. Times New Roman is a workhorse font that's been successful for a reason.

Yet it's an open question whether its longevity is attributable to its quality or merely to its ubiquity. Helvetica still inspires enough affection to have been the subject of a 2007 documentary feature. Times New Roman, meanwhile, has not attracted similar acts of homage.

Why not? Fame has a dark side. When Times New Roman appears in a book, document, or advertisement, it connotes apathy. It says, "I submitted to the font of least resistance." Times New Roman is not a font choice so much as the absence of a font choice, like the blackness of deep space is not a color. To look at Times New Roman is to gaze into the void. (This page is set in Times New Roman.)

If you have a choice about using Times New Roman, please stop. Use something else. See FONT SAMPLES for other options.

Did you make your business cards and letterhead at your local copy shop? No, you didn't, because you didn't want them to look shoddy and cheap. If you cared enough to avoid the copy shop, then you care enough to avoid Times New Roman. Times New Roman connotes apathy. You are not apathetic.

If you don't have a choice about using Times New Roman, make Times New Roman look its best. Both Windows 7 and Mac OS X now ship with Monotype's Times New Roman. Monotype offers additional styles in the Times New Roman family that will improve its versatility and appearance, like small caps and additional weights (see page 118).

The origin of the Times New Roman design has always been a bit mysterious. Stanley Morison was certainly familiar with 16th-century French typographer Robert Granjon, whose work has been said to be a starting point for Times New Roman.

But its more direct ancestor is probably Plantin, another Monotype font, designed in 1914 by Frank Pierpont. (This column is set in Plantin.) Plantin was also based on Granjon's work. Seen side by side, the resemblance is unmistakable: Times New Roman is a taller, brighter version of Plantin.

Or is it? Typographer Mike Parker discovered that in the early 1900s—before Times New Roman or Plantin existed—Boston yacht builder William Starling Burgess drew samples of a new font and sent them to Monotype's U.S. affiliate. Burgess lost interest in the project, but his drawings were never returned. Parker theorizes that years later, Burgess's drawings were passed along to Morison, who used them as the basis of Times New Roman.

Parker's theory is based in part on his examination of Burgess's drawings, which are archived at the Smithsonian. Parker created a new font family from these drawings—and the result is uncannily similar to Times New Roman. In honor of Burgess, Parker named the font Starling. (This column is set in Starling.)

Parker's theory is controversial among some font historians because it implies that Morison appropriated someone else's work without credit. It may also be controversial because Parker was Linotype's typographic director for 20 years.

But these criticisms are a little silly. Just about every font design is the product of new ideas mixed with old ideas—some acknowledged, some not. As with any creative endeavor, the line between acceptable influence and unethical appropriation is often subjective.

Moreover, as time passes and memories fade, it's increasingly unlikely that the parentage of Times New Roman will ever be conclusively determined.

These days, writers and other font users can choose from numerous alternatives to Times New Roman that share its essential flavor but avoid its shortcomings (including one I designed, called Equity). If you're a diehard fan of Times New Roman, consider them (see page 118).

Romanesque — PLANTIN

Romanesque — TIMES

Romanesque — STARLING

Font samples

Fonts are only one ingredient of typography. And great fonts are neither necessary nor sufficient for great typography. It's possible to produce professional-level typography with SYSTEM FONTS. It's also possible to produce awful typography with professional fonts.

That's why this chapter appears in the middle of the book rather than at the beginning. Don't rely on professional fonts as a substitute for the fundamentals of TYPE COMPOSITION and TEXT FORMATTING. But also don't overlook professional fonts as an easy, cost-effective typographic upgrade for your documents.

WHAT ARE FONTS?

Fonts are not programs that run software code, like your word processor or web browser. They are static data files, like MP3s or PDFs. Each font file contains information that defines the shapes of the letters, spacing, KERNING, and other miscellany. There's one font file for each style in the family. (A *style* means one visual variant, like roman, italic, bold, etc.)

Most professional fonts are delivered in the OpenType format. Some are offered in the older TrueType format. OpenType and TrueType files can be used on either Windows or the Mac.

WHY USE PROFESSIONAL FONTS?

The best professional fonts are better than any system font—and in ways that everyone, even people who think they don't have an eye for typography, can appreciate. Though you can't have the world's best typographers lay out your documents, you can incorporate their work into your documents with a font.

Professional fonts are also a great value. Yes, they cost money. But you can get a top-quality font family for under $200. These fonts will improve the appearance of every document you create, they're distinctive, they will never break, they won't go obsolete in three years, and they won't need to be upgraded. Best of all, you can put them to work without learning anything new.

HOW THESE SAMPLES ARE ORGANIZED

In this section, I've started with the most common system fonts and picked professional fonts that would make good substitutes. Each sample page contains four fonts.

The system font appears at the top.

The second font is a baby step—a professional font that's as close as possible to the system font, but still a worthwhile improvement.

The third font is visibly different than the system font but incorporates similar visual themes.

The fourth font is even more different, but would still make a good substitute for the system font.

Each font has a code attached to it. These codes will take you to PDF sample documents on the Typography for Lawyers website and information on how to get the font. To use a code, go to:

`http://typographyforlawyers.com/code/`

Enter the code number in the box that appears.

This section is not exhaustive or exclusive. The BIBLIOGRAPHY includes books that go into more depth about the kinds of professional fonts available and how they differ from each other.

HOW TO BUY FONTS

Fonts are sold online. You can buy fonts either direct from the websites of font designers, or from retailers who sell fonts from many designers. There's not much difference in price, which is in the range of $20–50 per style. After you pay, you download the fonts and install them.

For BODY TEXT, the core styles you will want are roman, italic, bold, bold italic, and roman small caps.

ABOUT FONT NAMES

Another reason to use the *Typography for Lawyers* web codes: they're guaranteed to take you to the exact fonts mentioned here.

Font names are confusing, even for professional typographers. Names of contemporary fonts (e.g., Myriad, Minion) are trademarked, so their names are distinct. But names of long-dead typographers (e.g., Baskerville, Garamond, Caslon) are not protected, and their names get included in many font names whether the association is apt or not.

The name of a dead typographer says nothing about the quality of the font nor how it appears on the page. For instance, Stempel Garamond and ITC Garamond are about as similar as Bart Simpson and Lisa Simpson.

To further complicate the picture, some fonts with trademarked names (e.g., Helvetica, Palatino) have been revised and released under slightly different names (e.g., Helvetica Neue, Palatino Nova). Pay attention to the full name.

HOW TO INSTALL (OR REMOVE) FONTS

WINDOWS | *All versions of Windows since XP use the same procedure. Go to the ‹Start› menu ➔ ‹Control Panel› ➔ ‹Fonts›. This will open a folder with all your installed fonts. Drag your new fonts into this folder. (To remove fonts, delete font files from this same folder.)*

MAC | *In the ‹Applications› folder, launch ‹Font Book›. Drag your new fonts into the font list. (To remove fonts, delete fonts from the list.)*

HOW TO USE FONTS

Once installed, new fonts show up in your font menu along with the usual system fonts. Use them the same way.

RESPECT YOUR LICENSE

Fonts are software. Like most software, fonts are offered under a license. Fonts are usually licensed per user. The most common way font licenses are violated is when someone buys a single-user license and then shares it with others in the organization.

Please—be a good typographic citizen. Buy the number of licenses you need and follow the license terms.

DISCLOSURE

I have no financial stake in any of the fonts shown here, except the ones I designed—FB Alix, Concourse, and Equity.

Arial

Robin Nicholas &
Patricia Saunders
1982
Monotype Imaging
Code 11601

ABCDEFGHIJ
KLMNOPQRS
TUVWXYZ&
abcdefghijk
lmnopqrstu
vwxyz!?¶§
0123456789

WE THE PEOPLE OF THE UNITED
States, in Order to form a more perfect Union,
establish Justice, insure domestic Tranquility,
provide for the common defense, promote the
general Welfare, and secure the Blessings of
Liberty to ourselves and our Posterity,
do ordain and establish this Constitution.

ITC Franklin Gothic

M.F. Benton & V. Caruso
1902
ITC / Monotype Imaging
Code 11602

ABCDEFGHIJ
KLMNOPQRS
TUVWXYZ&
abcdefghijk
lmnopqrstu
vwxyz!?¶§
0123456789

WE THE PEOPLE OF THE UNITED
States, in Order to form a more perfect Union,
establish Justice, insure domestic Tranquility,
provide for the common defense, promote the
general Welfare, and secure the Blessings of
Liberty to ourselves and our Posterity,
do ordain and establish this Constitution.

Atlas

K. Bernau, S. Carvalho,
& C. Schwartz
2012
Linotype
Code 11605

ABCDEFGHIJ
KLMNOPQRS
TUVWXYZ&
abcdefghijk
lmnopqrstu
vwxyz!?¶§
0123456789

WE THE PEOPLE OF THE UNITED
States, in Order to form a more perfect Union,
establish Justice, insure domestic Tranquility,
provide for the common defense, promote the
general Welfare, and secure the Blessings of
Liberty to ourselves and our Posterity,
do ordain and establish this Constitution.

Syntax

Hans Eduard Meier
1968
Linotype
Code 11604

ABCDEFGHIJ
KLMNOPQRS
TUVWXYZ&
abcdefghijk
lmnopqrstu
vwxyz!?¶§
0123456789

WE THE PEOPLE OF THE UNITED
States, in Order to form a more perfect Union,
establish Justice, insure domestic Tranquility,
provide for the common defense, promote the
general Welfare, and secure the Blessings of
Liberty to ourselves and our Posterity,
do ordain and establish this Constitution.

When sans serif fonts emerged in the 19th century, they were used mostly at headline sizes, not BODY TEXT sizes. But modern typography uses sans serifs at all sizes. Designs like **ARIAL** and Helvetica were meant to be comfortable for extended reading.

I detest Arial (see page 84 for why), but **ITC FRANKLIN GOTHIC** and **SYNTAX** are excellent alternatives—well-established sans serifs that are familiar but not mundane. **ATLAS** is a new design, but one rooted in the midcentury tradition.

Helvetica

Max Miedinger
1957
Linotype
Code 11701

ABCDEFGHIJ
KLMNOPQRS
TUVWXYZ&
abcdefghijk
lmnopqrstu
vwxyz!?¶§
0123456789

WE THE PEOPLE OF THE UNITED
States, in Order to form a more perfect Union,
establish Justice, insure domestic Tranquility,
provide for the common defense, promote the
general Welfare, and secure the Blessings of
Liberty to ourselves and our Posterity,
do ordain and establish this Constitution.

Neue Haas Grotesk

Christian Schwartz
2011
Linotype
Code 11705

ABCDEFGHIJ
KLMNOPQRS
TUVWXYZ&
abcdefghijk
lmnopqrstu
vwxyz!?¶§
0123456789

WE THE PEOPLE OF THE UNITED
States, in Order to form a more perfect Union,
establish Justice, insure domestic Tranquility,
provide for the common defense, promote the
general Welfare, and secure the Blessings of
Liberty to ourselves and our Posterity,
do ordain and establish this Constitution.

Frutiger

Adrian Frutiger
1976
Linotype
Code 11703

ABCDEFGHIJ
KLMNOPQRS
TUVWXYZ&
abcdefghijk
lmnopqrstu
vwxyz!?¶§
0123456789

WE THE PEOPLE OF THE UNITED
States, in Order to form a more perfect Union,
establish Justice, insure domestic Tranquility,
provide for the common defense, promote the
general Welfare, and secure the Blessings of
Liberty to ourselves and our Posterity,
do ordain and establish this Constitution.

Concourse

Matthew Butterick
2012
MB Type
Code 11706

ABCDEFGHIJ
KLMNOPQRS
TUVWXYZ&
abcdefghijk
lmnopqrstu
vwxyz!?¶§
0123456789

WE THE PEOPLE OF THE UNITED
States, in Order to form a more perfect Union,
establish Justice, insure domestic Tranquility,
provide for the common defense, promote the
general Welfare, and secure the Blessings of
Liberty to ourselves and our Posterity,
do ordain and establish this Constitution.

HELVETICA is an example of what I would call a "neutral" sans serif font, designed to be plain and informational. If you like Helvetica, try **NEUE HAAS GROTESK,** the first digital version that captures the subtlety of the 1957 original. If you're less attached to Helvetica, try **FRUTIGER**, another classic sans serif design. My newest font family, **CONCOURSE**, was influenced by sans serifs of the 1930s, and is used throughout this book. It also makes a good companion for Equity (see next page).

Times New Roman

S. Morison & V. Lardent
1932
Monotype Imaging
Code 11801

ABCDEFGHIJ
KLMNOPQRS
TUVWXYZ&
abcdefghijk
lmnopqrstu
vwxyz!?¶§
0123456789

WE THE PEOPLE OF THE UNITED States, in Order to form a more perfect Union, establish Justice, insure domestic Tranquility, provide for the common defense, promote the *general Welfare, and secure the Blessings of* **Liberty to ourselves and our Posterity,** do ordain and establish this Constitution.

Starling

William Starling Burgess
& Mike Parker
2009
Font Bureau
Code 11803

ABCDEFGHIJ
KLMNOPQRS
TUVWXYZ&
abcdefghijk
lmnopqrstu
vwxyz!?¶§
0123456789

WE THE PEOPLE OF THE UNITED States, in Order to form a more perfect Union, establish Justice, insure domestic Tranquility, provide for the common defense, promote the *general Welfare, and secure the Blessings of* **Liberty to ourselves and our Posterity,** do ordain and establish this Constitution.

Plantin

Frank Pierpont
1914
Monotype Imaging
Code 11802

ABCDEFGHIJ
KLMNOPQRS
TUVWXYZ&
abcdefghijk
lmnopqrstu
vwxyz!?¶§
0123456789

WE THE PEOPLE OF THE UNITED States, in Order to form a more perfect Union, establish Justice, insure domestic Tranquility, provide for the common defense, promote the *general Welfare, and secure the Blessings of* **Liberty to ourselves and our Posterity,** do ordain and establish this Constitution.

Equity

Matthew Butterick
2011
MB Type
Code 11806

ABCDEFGHIJ
KLMNOPQRS
TUVWXYZ&
abcdefghijk
lmnopqrstu
vwxyz!?¶§
0123456789

WE THE PEOPLE OF THE UNITED States, in Order to form a more perfect Union, establish Justice, insure domestic Tranquility, provide for the common defense, promote the *general Welfare, and secure the Blessings of* **Liberty to ourselves and our Posterity,** do ordain and establish this Constitution.

If you like good old **TIMES NEW ROMAN**, investigate the other styles (e.g., semibold, small caps) available from Monotype Imaging. **STARLING** and **PLANTIN** are based on the work of two designers who likely influenced Times New Roman (see page 110).

Compared to Times New Roman, Plantin is less compressed horizontally, and Starling has an appealing hand-finished quality. **EQUITY** is a text family I designed for lawyers. It fits as much text on the page as Times New Roman, but adds heft and authority.

Palatino

Hermann Zapf
1948
Linotype
Code 11901

ABCDEFGHIJ
KLMNOPQRS
TUVWXYZ&
abcdefghijk
lmnopqrstu
vwxyz!?¶§
0123456789

WE THE PEOPLE OF THE UNITED
States, in Order to form a more perfect Union,
establish Justice, insure domestic Tranquility,
provide for the common defense, promote the
general Welfare, and secure the Blessings of
Liberty to ourselves and our Posterity,
do ordain and establish this Constitution.

Palatino Nova

H. Zapf & A. Kobayashi
2005
Linotype
Code 11902

ABCDEFGHIJ
KLMNOPQRS
TUVWXYZ&
abcdefghijk
lmnopqrstu
vwxyz!?¶§
0123456789

WE THE PEOPLE OF THE UNITED
States, in Order to form a more perfect Union,
establish Justice, insure domestic Tranquility,
provide for the common defense, promote the
general Welfare, and secure the Blessings of
Liberty to ourselves and our Posterity,
do ordain and establish this Constitution.

Bembo Book

Monotype staff
1929 / 2005
Monotype Imaging
Code 11804

ABCDEFGHIJ
KLMNOPQRS
TUVWXYZ&
abcdefghijk
lmnopqrstu
vwxyz!?¶§
0123456789

WE THE PEOPLE OF THE UNITED
States, in Order to form a more perfect Union,
establish Justice, insure domestic Tranquility,
provide for the common defense, promote the
general Welfare, and secure the Blessings of
Liberty to ourselves and our Posterity,
do ordain and establish this Constitution.

Iowan Old Style

John Downer
1990
Bitstream
Code 11905

ABCDEFGHIJ
KLMNOPQRS
TUVWXYZ&
abcdefghijk
lmnopqrstu
vwxyz!?¶§
0123456789

WE THE PEOPLE OF THE UNITED
States, in Order to form a more perfect Union,
establish Justice, insure domestic Tranquility,
provide for the common defense, promote the
general Welfare, and secure the Blessings of
Liberty to ourselves and our Posterity,
do ordain and establish this Constitution.

PALATINO is the work of Hermann Zapf, who is a calligrapher by training. Many of his fonts reflect this influence. But the Palatino SYSTEM FONT is a harsh representation of Zapf's original design. PALATINO NOVA is Zapf's own reworking of Palatino that restores its original fluid subtlety. BEMBO BOOK is a revision of the famous 1929 Monotype face, which was itself based on Italian Renaissance typography. Despite the name, so was IOWAN OLD STYLE, but it's a looser interpretation of that model.

Courier New

Monotype staff
1990
Monotype Imaging
Code 12001

ABCDEFGHIJ
KLMNOPQRS
TUVWXYZ&
abcdefghijk
lmnopqrstu
vwxyz!?¶§
0123456789

WE THE PEOPLE OF THE UNITED States, in Order to form a more perfect Union, establish Justice, insure domestic Tranquility, provide *for the common defense, promote the* **general Welfare, and secure the** Blessings of Liberty to ourselves and our Posterity, do ordain and establish this Constitution.

Courier 10 Pitch

Howard Kettler
1956
Bitstream
Code 12002

ABCDEFGHIJ
KLMNOPQRS
TUVWXYZ&
abcdefghijk
lmnopqrstu
vwxyz!?¶§
0123456789

WE THE PEOPLE OF THE UNITED States, in Order to form a more perfect Union, establish Justice, insure domestic Tranquility, provide *for the common defense, promote the* **general Welfare, and secure the** Blessings of Liberty to ourselves and our Posterity, do ordain and establish this Constitution.

FB Alix

Matthew Butterick
2011
Font Bureau
Code 12003

ABCDEFGHIJ
KLMNOPQRS
TUVWXYZ&
abcdefghijk
lmnopqrstu
vwxyz!?¶§
0123456789

WE THE PEOPLE OF THE UNITED States, in Order to form a more perfect Union, establish Justice, insure domestic Tranquility, provide *for the common defense*, *promote the* **general Welfare, and secure the** Blessings of Liberty to ourselves and our Posterity, do ordain and establish this Constitution.

I'm in an awkward position. As your typography advisor, I've counseled you not to use MONO-SPACED FONTS. But the truth is—I really like them. The golden age of monospaced fonts was probably the 1950s, when IBM led the typewriter industry and released a series of great monospaced designs. One of these was Courier. But the system font **COURIER NEW** is a beastly imitation of the original: spindly, lumpy, and just plain ugly. **COURIER 10 PITCH** is a better rendition of the original Courier design. In honor of this book, I've created **FB ALIX**, a monospaced font family influenced by several typewriter fonts of the '50s, and optimized for BODY TEXT. FB Alix has a feature that's very rare among monospaced fonts: a genuine italic, instead of a sloped roman like Courier.

Georgia

Matthew Carter
1996
Microsoft
Code 12101

ABCDEFGHIJ
KLMNOPQRS
TUVWXYZ&
abcdefghijk
lmnopqrstu
vwxyz!?¶§
0123456789

WE THE PEOPLE OF THE UNITED States, in Order to form a more perfect Union, establish Justice, insure domestic Tranquility, provide for the common defense, promote the *general Welfare, and secure the Blessings of* **Liberty to ourselves and our Posterity,** do ordain and establish this Constitution.

Miller

Matthew Carter
1997
Carter & Cone Type /
Font Bureau
Code 12102

ABCDEFGHIJ
KLMNOPQRS
TUVWXYZ&
abcdefghijk
lmnopqrstu
vwxyz!?¶§
0123456789

WE THE PEOPLE OF THE UNITED States, in Order to form a more perfect Union, establish Justice, insure domestic Tranquility, provide for the common defense, promote the *general Welfare, and secure the Blessings of* **Liberty to ourselves and our Posterity,** do ordain and establish this Constitution.

Harriet

Jackson Cavanaugh
2012
Okay Type Foundry
Code 12105

ABCDEFGHIJ
KLMNOPQRS
TUVWXYZ&
abcdefghijk
lmnopqrstu
vwxyz!?¶§
0123456789

WE THE PEOPLE OF THE UNITED States, in Order to form a more perfect Union, establish Justice, insure domestic Tranquility, provide for the common defense, promote the *general Welfare, and secure the Blessings of* **Liberty to ourselves and our Posterity,** do ordain and establish this Constitution.

Lyon

Kai Bernau
2009
Commercial Type
Code 12104

ABCDEFGHIJ
KLMNOPQRS
TUVWXYZ&
abcdefghijk
lmnopqrstu
vwxyz!?¶§
0123456789

WE THE PEOPLE OF THE UNITED States, in Order to form a more perfect Union, establish Justice, insure domestic Tranquility, provide for the common defense, promote the *general Welfare, and secure the Blessings of* **Liberty to ourselves and our Posterity,** do ordain and establish this Constitution.

GEORGIA was designed primarily to work well on screen. The compromise is that it can be clunky on the printed page. MILLER shares Georgia's DNA but it's more subtle and detailed, making it preferable to Georgia for print use. (See a larger-size comparison on page 82.) Like Miller, HARRIET and LYON are based on historical models but with a contemporary spin, making them a nice blend of traditional and modern. Lyon is used for BODY TEXT in this book; Harriet is used for chapter headings.

Verdana

Matthew Carter
1996
Microsoft
Code 12201

ABCDEFGHIJ
KLMNOPQRS
TUVWXYZ&
abcdefghijk
lmnopqrstu
vwxyz!?¶§
0123456789

WE THE PEOPLE OF THE UNITED States, in Order to form a more perfect Union, establish Justice, insure domestic Tranquility, provide for the common defense, promote the *general Welfare, and secure the Blessings of* **Liberty to ourselves and our Posterity,** do ordain and establish this Constitution.

Alright Sans

Jackson Cavanaugh
2009
Okay Type Foundry
Code 12205

ABCDEFGHIJ
KLMNOPQRS
TUVWXYZ&
abcdefghijk
lmnopqrstu
vwxyz!?¶§
0123456789

WE THE PEOPLE OF THE UNITED States, in Order to form a more perfect Union, establish Justice, insure domestic Tranquility, provide for the common defense, promote the *general Welfare, and secure the Blessings of* **Liberty to ourselves and our Posterity,** do ordain and establish this Constitution.

Amplitude

Christian Schwartz
2003
Font Bureau
Code 12203

ABCDEFGHIJ
KLMNOPQRS
TUVWXYZ&
abcdefghijk
lmnopqrstu
vwxyz!?¶§
0123456789

WE THE PEOPLE OF THE UNITED States, in Order to form a more perfect Union, establish Justice, insure domestic Tranquility, provide for the common defense, promote the **general Welfare, and secure the Blessings of** **Liberty to ourselves and our Posterity,** do ordain and establish this Constitution.

Colfax

Eric Olson
2012
Process Type Foundry
Code 12206

ABCDEFGHIJ
KLMNOPQRS
TUVWXYZ&
abcdefghijk
lmnopqrstu
vwxyz!?¶§
0123456789

WE THE PEOPLE OF THE UNITED States, in Order to form a more perfect Union, establish Justice, insure domestic Tranquility, provide for the common defense, promote the *general Welfare, and secure the Blessings of* **Liberty to ourselves and our Posterity,** do ordain and establish this Constitution.

VERDANA was designed for the screen, so it's great for websites. For printed material, it's not so great. **ALRIGHT SANS**, **AMPLITUDE**, and **COLFAX** are sans serifs that work well in print. Alright is called a *humanist* sans serif because it relies on the proportions of traditional serif fonts. Amplitude draws from the spirit of *agates*, newspaper fonts designed to be readable at very small sizes (so it works especially well on BUSINESS CARDS). Colfax is called a *geometric* sans serif because it's built on basic mathematical shapes.

Gill Sans

Eric Gill
1928
Monotype Imaging
Code 12301

ABCDEFGHIJ
KLMNOPQRS
TUVWXYZ&
abcdefghijk
lmnopqrstu
vwxyz!?¶§
0123456789

WE THE PEOPLE OF THE UNITED
States, in Order to form a more perfect Union,
establish Justice, insure domestic Tranquility,
provide for the common defense, promote the
general Welfare, and secure the Blessings of
Liberty to ourselves and our Posterity,
do ordain and establish this Constitution.

Mr Eaves

Zuzana Licko
2009
Emigre
Code 12302

ABCDEFGHIJ
KLMNOPQRS
TUVWXYZ&
abcdefghijk
lmnopqrstu
vwxyz!?¶§
0123456789

WE THE PEOPLE OF THE UNITED
States, in Order to form a more perfect Union,
establish Justice, insure domestic Tranquility,
provide for the common defense, promote the
general Welfare, and secure the Blessings of
Liberty to ourselves and our Posterity,
do ordain and establish this Constitution.

FF Scala Sans

Martin Majoor
1992
FSI FontShop Int'l
Code 12303

ABCDEFGHIJ
KLMNOPQRS
TUVWXYZ&
abcdefghijk
lmnopqrstu
vwxyz!?¶§
0123456789

WE THE PEOPLE OF THE UNITED
States, in Order to form a more perfect Union,
establish Justice, insure domestic Tranquility,
provide for the common defense, promote the
general Welfare, and secure the Blessings of
Liberty to ourselves and our Posterity,
do ordain and establish this Constitution.

FF Quadraat Sans

Fred Smeijers
1997
FSI FontShop Int'l
Code 12304

ABCDEFGHIJ
KLMNOPQRS
TUVWXYZ&
abcdefghijk
lmnopqrstu
vwxyz!?¶§
0123456789

WE THE PEOPLE OF THE UNITED
States, in Order to form a more perfect Union,
establish Justice, insure domestic Tranquility,
provide for the common defense, promote the
general Welfare, and secure the Blessings of
Liberty to ourselves and our Posterity,
do ordain and establish this Constitution.

I complain a lot about SYSTEM FONTS but I won't say a bad word about GILL SANS—it's overexposed, but it hasn't worn out its welcome. (With me, at least.) Gill Sans lit the way for other sans serif fonts that combine geometric precision with looser hand-drawn features, though many fail to find the right balance. MR EAVES, FF SCALA SANS, and FF QUADRAAT SANS are successful. Quadraat Sans appears on the cover of this book.

Cambria

Jelle Bosma
2004
Microsoft
Code 12401

ABCDEFGHIJ
KLMNOPQRS
TUVWXYZ&
abcdefghijk
lmnopqrstu
vwxyz!?¶§
0123456789

WE THE PEOPLE OF THE UNITED
States, in Order to form a more perfect Union,
establish Justice, insure domestic Tranquility,
provide for the common defense, promote the
general Welfare, and secure the Blessings of
Liberty to ourselves and our Posterity,
do ordain and establish this Constitution.

Guardian

Paul Barnes &
Christian Schwartz
2005
Commercial Type
Code 12402

ABCDEFGHIJ
KLMNOPQRS
TUVWXYZ&
abcdefghijk
lmnopqrstu
vwxyz!?¶§
0123456789

WE THE PEOPLE OF THE UNITED
States, in Order to form a more perfect Union,
establish Justice, insure domestic Tranquility,
provide for the common defense, promote the
general Welfare, and secure the Blessings of
Liberty to ourselves and our Posterity,
do ordain and establish this Constitution.

Elena

Nicole Dotin
2011
Process Type Foundry
Code 12405

ABCDEFGHIJ
KLMNOPQRS
TUVWXYZ&
abcdefghijk
lmnopqrstu
vwxyz!?¶§
0123456789

WE THE PEOPLE OF THE UNITED
States, in Order to form a more perfect Union,
establish Justice, insure domestic Tranquility,
provide for the common defense, promote the
general Welfare, and secure the Blessings of
Liberty to ourselves and our Posterity,
do ordain and establish this Constitution.

FF Tisa

Mitja Miklavčič
2008
FSI FontShop Int'l
Code 12404

ABCDEFGHIJ
KLMNOPQRS
TUVWXYZ&
abcdefghijk
lmnopqrstu
vwxyz!?¶§
0123456789

WE THE PEOPLE OF THE UNITED
States, in Order to form a more perfect Union,
establish Justice, insure domestic Tranquility,
provide for the common defense, promote the
general Welfare, and secure the Blessings of
Liberty to ourselves and our Posterity,
do ordain and establish this Constitution.

It's counterintuitive, but a well-designed font can have a lot of subtle variation between letters and still look consistent on the page. The converse of this principle is that a font with too much consistency can be numbing to read. **CAMBRIA** is an example of this problem. It works well on screen, but on the printed page, it induces headaches. **GUARDIAN** and **ELENA** are similar to Cambria but avoid monotony. **FF TISA** has a more relaxed, informal rhythm.

Calibri

Lucas de Groot
2007
Microsoft
Code 12501

ABCDEFGHIJ
KLMNOPQRS
TUVWXYZ&
abcdefghijk
lmnopqrstu
vwxyz!?¶§
0123456789

WE THE PEOPLE OF THE UNITED
States, in Order to form a more perfect Union,
establish Justice, insure domestic Tranquility,
provide for the common defense, promote the
general Welfare, and secure the Blessings of
Liberty to ourselves and our Posterity,
do ordain and establish this Constitution.

Whitney

Hoefler & Frere-Jones
2004
Hoefler & Frere-Jones
Code 12505

ABCDEFGHIJ
KLMNOPQRS
TUVWXYZ&
abcdefghijk
lmnopqrstu
vwxyz!?¶§
0123456789

WE THE PEOPLE OF THE UNITED
States, in Order to form a more perfect Union,
establish Justice, insure domestic Tranquility,
provide for the common defense, promote the
general Welfare, and secure the Blessings of
Liberty to ourselves and our Posterity,
do ordain and establish this Constitution.

Source Sans

Paul Hunt
2012
Adobe
Code 12506

ABCDEFGHIJ
KLMNOPQRS
TUVWXYZ&
abcdefghijk
lmnopqrstu
vwxyz!?¶§
0123456789

WE THE PEOPLE OF THE UNITED
States, in Order to form a more perfect Union,
establish Justice, insure domestic Tranquility,
provide for the common defense, promote the
general Welfare, and secure the Blessings of
Liberty to ourselves and our Posterity,
do ordain and establish this Constitution.

FF Meta

Erik Spiekermann
1991
FSI FontShop Int'l
Code 12502

ABCDEFGHIJ
KLMNOPQRS
TUVWXYZ&
abcdefghijk
lmnopqrstu
vwxyz!?¶§
0123456789

WE THE PEOPLE OF THE UNITED
States, in Order to form a more perfect Union,
establish Justice, insure domestic Tranquility,
provide for the common defense, promote the
general Welfare, and secure the Blessings of
Liberty to ourselves and our Posterity,
do ordain and establish this Constitution.

CALIBRI does its job better than Cambria, though it's still better on screen than in print. The rounded corners of the letters make text printed in Calibri seem soft. For a clean, slightly narrow sans serif font, you have better options. **WHITNEY** and **SOURCE SANS** both take inspiration from the famous 1908 face News Gothic. And you can't argue with the price of Source Sans: it's free. **FF META** has been hugely popular since its release, for good reason—it's versatile and attractive.

Baskerville

Monotype staff
1923
Monotype Imaging
Code 12601

ABCDEFGHIJ
KLMNOPQRS
TUVWXYZ&
abcdefghijk
lmnopqrstu
vwxyz!?¶§
0123456789

WE THE PEOPLE OF THE UNITED
States, in Order to form a more perfect Union,
establish Justice, insure domestic Tranquility,
provide for the common defense, promote the
general Welfare, and secure the Blessings of
Liberty to ourselves and our Posterity,
do ordain and establish this Constitution.

Baskerville 10

František Štorm
2009
Storm Type Foundry
Code 12602

ABCDEFGHIJ
KLMNOPQRS
TUVWXYZ&
abcdefghijk
lmnopqrstu
vwxyz!?¶§
0123456789

WE THE PEOPLE OF THE UNITED
States, in Order to form a more perfect Union,
establish Justice, insure domestic Tranquility,
provide for the common defense, promote the
general Welfare, and secure the Blessings of
Liberty to ourselves and our Posterity,
do ordain and establish this Constitution.

Mrs Eaves

Zuzana Licko
1996
Emigre
Code 12603

ABCDEFGHIJ
KLMNOPQRS
TUVWXYZ&
abcdefghijk
lmnopqrstu
vwxyz!?¶§
0123456789

WE THE PEOPLE OF THE UNITED
States, in Order to form a more perfect Union,
establish Justice, insure domestic Tranquility,
provide for the common defense, promote the
general Welfare, and secure the Blessings of
Liberty to ourselves and our Posterity,
do ordain and establish this Constitution.

Williams Caslon

William Berkson
2010
Font Bureau
Code 12604

ABCDEFGHIJ
KLMNOPQRS
TUVWXYZ&
abcdefghijk
lmnopqrstu
vwxyz!?¶§
0123456789

WE THE PEOPLE OF THE UNITED
States, in Order to form a more perfect Union,
establish Justice, insure domestic Tranquility,
provide for the common defense, promote the
general Welfare, and secure the Blessings of
Liberty to ourselves and our Posterity,
do ordain and establish this Constitution.

John Baskerville was an 18th-century English typographer whose work has inspired many fonts. But the **BASKERVILLE** system font is mediocre: brittle and excessively quaint. The best recreation of the traditional Baskerville look is **BASKERVILLE 10**. The definitive contemporary reinterpretation is **MRS EAVES**. William Caslon was a contemporary of Baskerville whose fonts were similarly sturdy and handsome. **WILLIAMS CASLON** captures these qualities well.

Hoefler Text

Hoefler & Frere-Jones
1991
Hoefler & Frere-Jones
Code 12701

ABCDEFGHIJ
KLMNOPQRS
TUVWXYZ&
abcdefghijk
lmnopqrstu
vwxyz!?¶§
0123456789

WE THE PEOPLE OF THE UNITED States, in Order to form a more perfect Union, establish Justice, insure domestic Tranquility, provide for the common defense, promote the *general Welfare, and secure the Blessings of* **Liberty to ourselves and our Posterity,** do ordain and establish this Constitution.

Verdigris

Mark van Bronkhorst
2003
MVB Fonts
Code 12705

ABCDEFGHIJ
KLMNOPQRS
TUVWXYZ&
abcdefghijk
lmnopqrstu
vwxyz!?¶§
0123456789

WE THE PEOPLE OF THE UNITED States, in Order to form a more perfect Union, establish Justice, insure domestic Tranquility, provide for the common defense, promote the *general Welfare, and secure the Blessings of* **Liberty to ourselves and our Posterity,** do ordain and establish this Constitution.

Stempel Garamond

Stempel staff
1925
Linotype
Code 12703

ABCDEFGHIJ
KLMNOPQRS
TUVWXYZ&
abcdefghijk
lmnopqrstu
vwxyz!?¶§
0123456789

WE THE PEOPLE OF THE UNITED States, in Order to form a more perfect Union, establish Justice, insure domestic Tranquility, provide for the common defense, promote the *general Welfare, and secure the Blessings of* **Liberty to ourselves and our Posterity,** do ordain and establish this Constitution.

Sabon

Jan Tschichold
1967
Linotype
Code 12704

ABCDEFGHIJ
KLMNOPQRS
TUVWXYZ&
abcdefghijk
lmnopqrstu
vwxyz!?¶§
0123456789

WE THE PEOPLE OF THE UNITED States, in Order to form a more perfect Union, establish Justice, insure domestic Tranquility, provide for the common defense, promote the *general Welfare, and secure the Blessings of* **Liberty to ourselves and our Posterity,** do ordain and establish this Constitution.

HOEFLER TEXT is perfectly nice, but the version included with the Mac omits the semibold and bold styles. The publisher, Hoefler & Frere-Jones, offers the full family. Hoefler Text was influenced by the traditional European text fonts that also inspired

VERDIGRIS, **STEMPEL GARAMOND**, and **SABON**. Stempel Garamond is by far my favorite "Garamond" font. I'm also a big fan of Sabon—its wide, legible italic makes citations look great. Verdigris is a recent design that embodies the same classic virtues.

Optima

Hermann Zapf
1958
Linotype
Code 12801

ABCDEFGHIJ
KLMNOPQRS
TUVWXYZ&
abcdefghijk
lmnopqrstu
vwxyz!?¶§
0123456789

WE THE PEOPLE OF THE UNITED
States, in Order to form a more perfect Union,
establish Justice, insure domestic Tranquility,
provide for the common defense, promote the
general Welfare, and secure the Blessings of
Liberty to ourselves and our Posterity,
do ordain and establish this Constitution.

Optima Nova

H. Zapf & A. Kobayashi
2002
Linotype
Code 12802

ABCDEFGHIJ
KLMNOPQRS
TUVWXYZ&
abcdefghijk
lmnopqrstu
vwxyz!?¶§
0123456789

WE THE PEOPLE OF THE UNITED
States, in Order to form a more perfect Union,
establish Justice, insure domestic Tranquility,
provide for the common defense, promote the
general Welfare, and secure the Blessings of
Liberty to ourselves and our Posterity,
do ordain and establish this Constitution.

Amira

Cyrus Highsmith
2004
Font Bureau
Code 12803

ABCDEFGHIJ
KLMNOPQRS
TUVWXYZ&
abcdefghijk
lmnopqrstu
vwxyz!?¶§
0123456789

WE THE PEOPLE OF THE UNITED
States, in Order to form a more perfect Union,
establish Justice, insure domestic Tranquility,
provide for the common defense, promote the
general Welfare, and secure the Blessings of
Liberty to ourselves and our Posterity,
do ordain and establish this Constitution.

Magma

Sumner Stone
2004
Stone Type Foundry
Code 12804

ABCDEFGHIJ
KLMNOPQRS
TUVWXYZ&
abcdefghijk
lmnopqrstu
vwxyz!?§
0123456789

WE THE PEOPLE OF THE UNITED
States, in Order to form a more perfect Union,
establish Justice, insure domestic Tranquility,
provide for the common defense, promote the
general Welfare, and secure the Blessings of
Liberty to ourselves and our Posterity,
do ordain and establish this Constitution.

OPTIMA, like Palatino, is the work of Hermann Zapf, and also shows the influence of pen-drawn letters. **OPTIMA NOVA** is Zapf's own reworking of the design, with improvements that include better italic styles—note the differences between the a, e, f, and g.

AMIRA is a recent design also influenced by pen lettering, though with a more angular feel than Optima. **MAGMA** is a hybrid of the pen-drawn and sans serif models, and it's jauntier than Optima and Amira.

Rockwell

Monotype staff
1934
Monotype Imaging
Code 12901

ABCDEFGHIJ
KLMNOPQRS
TUVWXYZ&
abcdefghijk
lmnopqrstu
vwxyz!?¶§
0123456789

WE THE PEOPLE OF THE UNITED
States, in Order to form a more perfect Union,
establish Justice, insure domestic Tranquility,
provide for the common defense, promote the
general Welfare, and secure the Blessings of
Liberty to ourselves and our Posterity,
do ordain and establish this Constitution.

Silica

Sumner Stone
1993
Stone Type Foundry
Code 12903

ABCDEFGHIJ
KLMNOPQRS
TUVWXYZ&
abcdefghijk
lmnopqrstu
vwxyz!?¶§
0123456789

WE THE PEOPLE OF THE UNITED
States, in Order to form a more perfect Union,
establish Justice, insure domestic Tranquility,
provide for the common defense, promote the
general Welfare, and secure the Blessings of
Liberty to ourselves and our Posterity,
do ordain and establish this Constitution.

Sentinel

Hoefler & Frere-Jones
2004
Hoefler & Frere-Jones
Code 12902

ABCDEFGHIJ
KLMNOPQRS
TUVWXYZ&
abcdefghijk
lmnopqrstu
vwxyz!?¶§
0123456789

WE THE PEOPLE OF THE UNITED
States, in Order to form a more perfect Union,
establish Justice, insure domestic Tranquility,
provide for the common defense, promote the
general Welfare, and secure the Blessings of
Liberty to ourselves and our Posterity,
do ordain and establish this Constitution.

Vista Slab

Xavier Dupré
2008
Emigre
Code 12904

ABCDEFGHIJ
KLMNOPQRS
TUVWXYZ&
abcdefghijk
lmnopqrstu
vwxyz!?¶§
0123456789

WE THE PEOPLE OF THE UNITED
States, in Order to form a more perfect Union,
establish Justice, insure domestic Tranquility,
provide for the common defense, promote the
general Welfare, and secure the Blessings of
Liberty to ourselves and our Posterity,
do ordain and establish this Constitution.

ROCKWELL is an example of a *slab-serif* font, so named because the serifs on the ends of the letters are thick and rectangular. Rockwell's not bad, but it's a little dated. Modern slab-serif designs are more subtle and versatile. **SENTINEL** is an updated version of the classic slab-serif look. **VISTA SLAB**, on the other hand, is assertively contemporary. **SILICA** falls in between. Slab serifs work well for display and short stretches of text. They also mix well with regular serif fonts, for example as HEADINGS.

Eldorado

William A. Dwiggins &
David Berlow
1997
Font Bureau
Code 13001

ABCDEFGHIJ
KLMNOPQRS
TUVWXYZ&
abcdefghijk
lmnopqrstu
vwxyz!?¶§
0123456789

WE THE PEOPLE OF THE UNITED
States, in Order to form a more perfect Union,
establish Justice, insure domestic Tranquility,
provide for the common defense, promote the
general Welfare, and secure the Blessings of
Liberty to ourselves and our Posterity,
do ordain and establish this Constitution.

FF Quadraat

Fred Smeijers
1992
FSI FontShop Int'l
Code 13002

ABCDEFGHIJ
KLMNOPQRS
TUVWXYZ&
abcdefghijk
lmnopqrstu
vwxyz!?¶§
0123456789

WE THE PEOPLE OF THE UNITED
States, in Order to form a more perfect Union,
establish Justice, insure domestic Tranquility,
provide for the common defense, promote the
general Welfare, and secure the Blessings of
Liberty to ourselves and our Posterity,
do ordain and establish this Constitution.

Ingeborg

Michael Hochleitner
2009
Typejockeys
Code 12103

ABCDEFGHIJ
KLMNOPQRS
TUVWXYZ&
abcdefghijk
lmnopqrstu
vwxyz!?¶§
0123456789

WE THE PEOPLE OF THE UNITED
States, in Order to form a more perfect Union,
establish Justice, insure domestic Tranquility,
provide for the common defense, promote the
general Welfare, and secure the Blessings of
Liberty to ourselves and our Posterity,
do ordain and establish this Constitution.

Tiempos

Kris Sowersby
2010
Klim Type Foundry
Code 11805

ABCDEFGHIJ
KLMNOPQRS
TUVWXYZ&
abcdefghijk
lmnopqrstu
vwxyz!?¶§
0123456789

WE THE PEOPLE OF THE UNITED
States, in Order to form a more perfect Union,
establish Justice, insure domestic Tranquility,
provide for the common defense, promote the
general Welfare, and secure the Blessings of
Liberty to ourselves and our Posterity,
do ordain and establish this Constitution.

A few more BODY TEXT fonts worth knowing about. **ELDORADO** is a lively design with an unusual feature: a separate "micro" style for very small text, like footnotes. **FF QUADRAAT** is a little like raw oysters: an acquired taste, but once you've tried it, there's nothing else like it. I'm a fan. **INGEBORG** and **TIEMPOS** are text fonts with a bright, contemporary finish. They both depart from traditional models, but remain comfortable to read.

Bodoni

Morris Fuller Benton
1911
Monotype Imaging

ABCDEFGHIJ
KLMNOPQRS
TUVWXYZ&
abcdefghijk
lmnopqrstu
vwxyz!?¶§
0123456789

WE THE PEOPLE OF TH[E UN]ITED States, in Order to form a more pe[rfect] Union, establish Justice, insure domestic Tra[nquili]ty, provide for the common defense, promo[te the] *general Welfare, and secure the Blessings of* **Liberty to ourselves and our Posterity,** do ordain and establish this Constitution.

FONTS TO AVOID

Bookman

Edward Benguiat
1975
Monotype Imaging

ABCDEFGHIJ
KLMNOPQRS
TUVWXYZ&
abcdefghijk
lmnopqrstu
vwxyz!?¶§
0123456789

WE THE PEOPLE OF THE UNITED States, in Order to form a more perfect Union, establish Justice, insure domestic Tranquility, provide for the common defense, promote the *general Welfare, and secure the Blessings of* **Liberty to ourselves and our Posterity,** do ordain and establish this Constitution.

COPPER-PLATE

Frederic Goudy
1901
Linotype

ABCDEFGHIJ
KLMNOPQRS
TUVWXYZ&
ABCDEFGHIJK
LMNOPQRSTU
VWXYZ!?¶§
0123456789

WE THE PEOPLE OF THE UNITED STATES, IN ORDER TO FORM A MORE PERFECT UNION, ESTABLISH JUSTICE, INSURE DOMESTIC TRANQUILITY, PROVIDE FOR THE COMMON **DEFENSE, PROMOTE THE GENERAL WELFARE, AND SECURE THE BLESSINGS OF LIBERTY TO** OURSELVES AND OUR POSTERITY, DO ORDAIN

Free fonts

All the time
All over the Internet

ABCDEFGHIJ
KLMNOPQRS
TUVWXYZ&
abcdefghijk
lmnopqrstu
vwxyz!?¶§
0123456789

WE THE PEOPLE OF THE UNITED States, in Order to form a more perfect Union, establish Justice, insure domestic Tranquility, provide for the common defense, promote the *general Welfare, and secure the Blessings of* **Liberty to ourselves and our Posterity,** do ordain and establish this Constitution.

And finally, some fonts to avoid. **BODONI** has very high contrast and isn't appealing at BODY TEXT sizes. **BOOKMAN** evokes the Ford administration. If fonts were clothing, this would be the corduroy suit. **COPPERPLATE** is a novelty design that's overstayed its welcome by forty or fifty years. **FREE FONTS** like Liberation Serif (shown above) fill a practical need for fonts without licensing restrictions. But in terms of design and craftsmanship, you usually get what you pay for. (One exception: Source Sans, on page 125.)

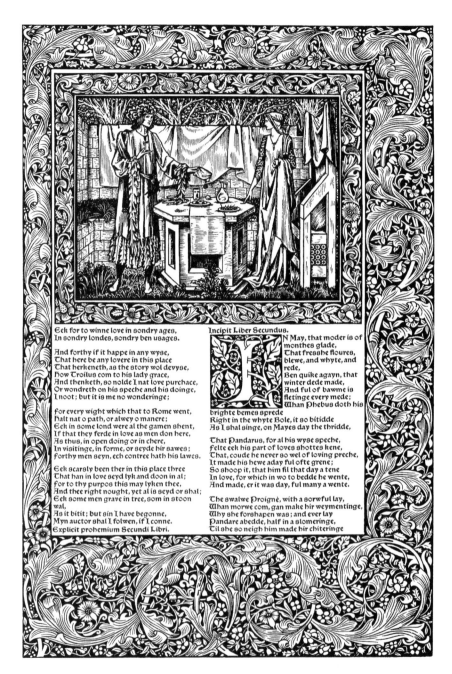

Eek for to winne love in sondry ages,
In sondry londes, sondry ben usages.

And forthy if it happe in any wyse,
That here be any lovere in this place
That herkeneth, as the story wol devyse,
How Troilus com to his lady grace,
And thenketh, so nolde I nat love purchace,
Or wondreth on his speche and his doinge,
I noot; but it is me no wonderinge;

For every wight which that to Rome went,
Halt nat o path, or alwey o manere;
Eek in some lond were al the gamen shent,
If that they ferde in love as men don here,
As thus, in open doing or in chere,
In visitinge, in forme, or seyde hir sawes;
Forthy men seyn, ech contree hath his lawes.

Eek scarsly been ther in this place three
That han in love seyd lyk and doon in al;
For to thy purpos this may lyken thee,
And thee right nought, yet al is seyd or shal;
Eek some men grave in tree, som in stoon wal,
As it bitit; but sin I have begonne,
Myn auctor shal I folwen, if I conne.
Explicit prohemium Secundi Libri.

Incipit Liber Secundus.

IN May, that moder is of monthes glade,
That fresshe floures, blewe, and whyte, and rede,
Ben quike agayn, that winter dede made,
And ful of bawme is fletinge every mede;
Whan Phebus doth his brighte bemes sprede
Right in the whyte Bole, it so bitidde
As I shal singe, on Mayes day the thridde,

That Pandarus, for al his wyse speche,
Felte eek his part of loves shottes kene,
That, coude he never so wel of loving preche,
It made his hewe aday ful ofte grene;
So shoop it, that him fil that day a tene
In love, for which in wo to bedde he wente,
And made, er it was day, ful many a wente.

The swalwe Proignè, with a sorwful lay,
Whan morwe com, gan make hir weymentinge,
Why she forshapen was; and ever lay
Pandare abedde, half in a slomeringe,
Til she so neigh him made hir chiteringe

ABOVE Page from the Kelmscott *Chaucer*, printed by William Morris, 1896.

Page layout

TYPE COMPOSITION WAS ABOUT PICK- ing the right characters. Text formatting was about the visual appearance of those characters. Page layout is about the positioning and relationship of text and other elements on the page.

In fine printing, typographers usually get to choose the page size of their documents. But you don't—most of the documents a lawyer creates will be on standard printer paper.

That's no reason to accept mediocrity. English artist and printer William Morris famously rebelled against mechanized, mass-produced typography—in the 1890s. He went on to produce a series of beautiful books intended as both a rebuke and an antidote to the increasingly coarse and industrialized ritual of printing.

Today, the struggle continues. Word processors beckon us with default settings and templates that promise great results with no effort.

But you only get out what you put in. Don't accept the defaults. You can do better.

Basic rules

centered text

It's boring— use sparingly

Centered text is overused. It's the typographic equivalent of vanilla ice cream—safe but boring. It's rare to see text centered in a book, newspaper, or magazine, except for the occasional headline or title. Asymmetry is nothing to fear.

Yet it is feared. So for all the fans of centered text, a poem:

An Ode to Centered Text

Centered text is acceptable when used for short phrases or titles,
like the name on your BUSINESS CARDS or LETTERHEAD.
Or in documents, you can center major section headings
like "Introduction," "Argument," and "Conclusion."
(It may be conventional in your jurisdiction
to center certain text in court filings.)
If you enjoy centering text, then
you should learn to use the
HARD LINE BREAK
so your lines start
in sensible
places.
OK?

Whole text blocks, including sentence-length headings in court filings, should not be centered. Centering makes text blocks difficult to read because both edges of the text block are uneven. Centered text blocks are also difficult to align with other page elements. See HEADINGS for better options.

Justified text is spaced so the left and right sides of the text block both have a clean edge. The usual alternative to justified text is *left-aligned text*, which has an uneven right edge. Compared to left-aligned text, justification gives text a cleaner, more formal look.

justified text

Acceptable but not mandatory

Justification works by adding white space between the words in each line so all the lines are the same length. This alters the ideal spacing of the font, but in paragraphs of reasonable width it's usually not distracting.

JUSTIFIED

Section 351 extends the time in which to file suit if the defendant was outside California when the action accrued or leaves the state after it accrued. It reads: "If, when the cause of action accrues against a person, he is out of the State, the action may be commenced

LEFT-ALIGNED

Section 351 extends the time in which to file suit if the defendant was outside California when the action accrued or leaves the state after it accrued. It reads: "If, when the cause of action accrues against a person, he is out of the State, the action may be commenced

If you're using justified text, you must also turn on HYPHENATION so you don't get gruesomely large spaces between words.

Notice that you can fit more words in less space with hyphenation turned on.

Section 351 extends the time in which to file suit if the defendant was outside California when the action accrued or leaves the state after it accrued. It reads: "If, when the cause of action accrues against a person, he is out of the State, the action may be commenced by

Section 351 extends the time in which to file suit if the defendant was outside California when the action accrued or leaves the state after it accrued. It reads: "If, when the cause of action accrues against a person, he is out of the State, the action may be

Justification is a matter of personal preference. It is not a signifier of professional typography. For instance, most major U.S. newspapers use a mix of justified and left-aligned text.

In my law practice, I almost never justify text. Why's that? The justification engine in a word processor is rudimentary compared to a professional page-layout program. I find that word-processor justification can make text look clunky and coarse. Left-aligning the text is more reliable.

Also, I don't like my documents to look dry and uninviting, even if the subject matter is. Left-aligning the text relaxes the page.

But the choice is yours.

first-line indents

Between one and four times the point size

A first-line indent is the most common way to signal the start of a new paragraph. The other common way is with SPACE BETWEEN PARAGRAPHS.

First-line indents and space between paragraphs have the same relationship as belts and suspenders. You only need one to get the job done. Using both is a mistake. If you use a first-line indent on a paragraph, don't use space between. And vice versa.

Typically, a first-line indent should be no smaller than the POINT SIZE of the text, otherwise it'll be hard to see. The indent should be no bigger than four times the point size, otherwise the first line will seem disconnected from the left edge of the text block. So a paragraph set in 12 point should have a first-line indent of 12–48 points. (Recall that there are 72 points to an inch, so this works out to 0.17–0.67 inches.)

But use your judgment—consider the width of the text block when setting the first-line indent. For instance, narrow text blocks (three inches or less) should have first-line indents toward the low end of this range. Wider text blocks should have bigger indents.

A first-line indent on the first paragraph of any text is optional, because it's obvious where the paragraph starts.

Drop caps are another option for the first paragraph—the first letter of the paragraph is enlarged so it descends three or four lines into the paragraph. Drop caps look pretentious and dorky in legal documents. You've been warned.

    The process server was denied entry to the defendant's home in the gated community known as Luxuria.   WRONG

            The process server was denied entry to the defendant's home in the gated community known as Luxuria.   WRONG

    The process server was denied entry to the defendant's home in the gated community known as Luxuria.   RIGHT

Don't use WORD SPACES or TABS to indent the first line—as you recall from WHITE-SPACE CHARACTERS, that's not what they're for. Paragraphs indented with word spaces or tabs are hard to keep consistent and difficult to reformat. Use the right tool for the job.

HOW TO SET A FIRST-LINE INDENT

WORD | *Right-click in the text and select* ‹Paragraph› ➡ ‹Indents and Spacing›. *Under* ‹Indentation›, *from the popup menu labeled* ‹Special›, *select* ‹First line› *and enter the measurement in the adjacent box.*

WORDPERFECT | ‹Format› ➡ ‹Paragraph› ➡ ‹Format›. *In the box next to* ‹First line indent›, *enter the measurement.*

PAGES | *Inspector (command + option + i)* ➜ *T icon in the top row (fourth from left)* ➜ *‹Tabs›. Under ‹Paragraph Indents›, in the box above ‹First Line›, enter the measurement.*

BY THE WAY

➜ It's possible to set a negative first-line indent, or *hanging indent*. Hanging indents are used in lists to create a rectangular text block with a list bullet that dangles off to the left. (As in this paragraph.) Avoid using a hanging indent without a bullet—your text block should not resemble Oklahoma. Text should only be indented inward.

space between paragraphs

Between four and ten points

Space between paragraphs is an alternative to a FIRST-LINE INDENT for signaling the start of a new paragraph.

The worst way to put space between paragraphs is to insert an extra carriage return. (See CARRIAGE RETURNS if you've forgotten why.)

As with first-line indents, you want the space to be large enough to be easily noticed, but not so large that the paragraphs seem disconnected. Four to ten points of space (0.06–0.14 inches) will usually suffice. The larger the POINT SIZE, the more space you'll need between paragraphs to make a visible difference.

HOW TO SET SPACE BETWEEN PARAGRAPHS

WORD | *Right-click in the text and select ‹Paragraph› ➜ ‹Indents and Spacing›. Under ‹Spacing›, in the box next to ‹After›, enter the measurement.*

WORDPERFECT | *‹Format› ➜ ‹Paragraph› ➜ ‹Format› ➜ ‹Spacing between paragraphs›. Select the button labeled ‹Distance in points›, and enter the measurement in the box.*

PAGES | *Inspector (command + option + i)* ➔ *T icon in the top row (fourth from left)* ➔ *‹Text›. Under ‹After Paragraph›, use the slider or the adjacent box to enter the measurement.*

BY THE WAY

➔ Is space before a paragraph equivalent to space after? Pretty much, because when you put two paragraphs of the same kind together, the total space between them equals the space after the first paragraph plus the space before the second paragraph. I prefer to use space after, and reserve space before for special circumstances. For instance, a BLOCK QUOTATION may need space before and after to look vertically aligned.

➔ Space between paragraphs is not the best choice for court filings with LINE NUMBERS. The only way to preserve the vertical alignment is to make the space between paragraphs equal to a whole line space. This leaves a lot of big gaps in the page and eats up your page limits. It can work with HEADINGS because a document contains fewer of them.

Line spacing is the vertical distance between lines of text. Most lawyers use either double-spaced lines or single-spaced lines—nothing in between.

These habits are held over from the typewriter era. Originally, a typewriter's carriage could only move vertically in units of a single line. Therefore, line-spacing choices were limited to one, two, or more lines at a time. Double-spacing became the default because single-spaced typewritten text is dense and hard to read. But double-spacing is still looser than optimal.

Most courts adopted their line-spacing standards in the typewriter era. That's why court rules usually call for double-spaced lines. (Notable exception: the United States Supreme Court.)

line spacing

120–145% of the point size

The traditional term for line spacing is **leading** (rhymes with **bedding**). Sometimes you see this term in typesetting software. Leading is so named because traditional print shops put strips of lead between lines of type to increase vertical space.

For most text, the optimal line spacing is between 120% and 145% of the point size. So if you're working with an 11-point font, use roughly 13–16 points of line spacing. (The text in this paragraph is set in 11 point with 12 points of line spacing, or 109% of the point size. It's too tight.)

For most text, the optimal line spacing is between 120% and 145% of the POINT SIZE. So if you're working with an 11-point font, use roughly 13–16 points of line spacing. (The text in this paragraph is set in 11 point with 15 points of line spacing, or 136% of the point size. It looks fine.)

For most text, the optimal line spacing is between 120% and 145% of the point size. So if you're working with an 11-point font, use roughly 13–16 points of line spacing. (The text in this paragraph is set in 11 point with 18 points of line spacing, or 164% of the point size. It's too loose.)

Word processors have a bewildering number of ways to set line spacing. Don't be thrown off—it all comes back to the same thing.

HOW TO SET LINE SPACING

If you prefer setting line height in inches rather than points, divide the point measurement by 72 (there are 72 points to an inch).

WORD | *Right-click in the text and select ‹Paragraph› from the menu. Go to the menu under ‹Line spacing›. ‹Exactly› is best—enter a fixed measurement. ‹Single›, ‹1.5 lines›, and ‹Double› are equivalent to about 117%, 175%, and 233% line spacing, contrary to what their names suggest. Don't use these—they miss the target zone of 120–145%. ‹Multiple› is also acceptable—enter line spacing as a decimal. To get line spacing in the 120–145% range, use a ‹Multiple› value of 1.03–1.24. (Not 1.20–1.45—as noted above, Word uses peculiar line-spacing math.) Never use ‹At least›, because that gives Word permission to adjust your line spacing unpredictably.*

WORDPERFECT | *‹Format› → ‹Line› → ‹Height› and ‹Spacing›. Line spacing in WordPerfect is the ‹Height› value multiplied by the ‹Spacing› value. (The benefit of this complication may be appreciated by WordPerfect fans, but is lost on me.) I recommend always leaving ‹Spacing› at 1.0 and* *just setting your line spacing with ‹Height›. Selecting ‹Height› lets you choose from ‹Fixed› or ‹At Least›. Use ‹Fixed›—enter a measurement in the 120–145% range. Don't use ‹At Least›.*

PAGES | *Inspector (command + option + i) → T icon in the top row (fourth from left) → ‹Text›. Under ‹Spacing› and ‹Line›, there's a slider. Find the popup menu next to the slider. ‹Exactly› is best—enter a fixed measurement. You can also use the ‹Multiple› option, but like Word, it adds extra space— about 17%. Therefore, to get line spacing in the 120–145% range, use a ‹Multiple› value of 1.03–1.29. Avoid the other options.*

BY THE WAY

→ Recall that different fonts set at the same point size may not appear the same size on the page. (See POINT SIZE for why.) A side effect is that fonts that run small will need less line spacing, and vice versa.

→ Line spacing has a much more significant effect on the **length** of a document than point size. If you need to fit a document onto a certain number of pages, try adjusting the line spacing first.

line length

45–90 characters or 2–3 alphabets

Line length is the distance between the left and right edges of a text block. Overly long lines are a common problem, but they're easy to correct. Shorter lines will make a big difference in the legibility and professionalism of your layout.

The most useful way to measure line length is by average **characters per line**. Measuring in inches or centimeters is less useful because the POINT SIZE of the font affects the number of characters per inch. Average characters per line works independently of point size.

Shorter lines are more comfortable to read than longer lines. As line length increases, your eye has to travel farther from the end of one line to the beginning of the next, making it harder to track your progress vertically.

Newspaper columns are very tall, so they also have to be very narrow to make vertical tracking easy.

Aim for an average line length of 45–90 characters, including spaces. You can check line length using word count.

HOW TO USE WORD COUNT

WORD 2003 | ‹Tools› ➜ ‹Word Count›

WORD 2007 & 2010 | ‹Review› ➜ ‹Proofing› *panel* ➜ ‹Word Count› *(icon looks like "ABC" above "123")*

WORDPERFECT | ‹Tools› ➜ ‹Word Count›

PAGES | ‹Edit› ➜ ‹Writing Tools› ➜ ‹Show Statistics›. *If text is selected in the document, the* ‹Range› *popup menu lets you toggle between word counts for the selection and for the whole document.*

Alternatively, use the alphabet test to set line length. You should be able to fit between two and three alphabets on your line, like so:

abcdefghijklmnopqrstuvwxyzabcdefghijklmnopqrstuvwxyzabcdef

|1 |2 |3

page margins

One inch is not enough

A **gutter** margin is extra space on one side of a page that accounts for a binding. In a duplex (two-sided) document, the gutter will automatically alternate sides.

Page margins set the default territory your text occupies on the page. Page margins determine the width of the text block, and thus have the greatest effect on LINE LENGTH. (POINT SIZE also affects line length, though more finely.) As page margins increase, line length decreases, and vice versa.

Most word processors default to page margins of one inch. On standard 8.5″× 11″ paper, that produces a line length of 6.5 inches. That's fine for MONOSPACED FONTS, which use a lot of horizontal space. But for proportional fonts, one-inch margins are too small.

At 12 point, left and right page margins of 1.5–2.0 inches will usually give you a comfortable line length. But don't take that range as an absolute—focus on getting the number of characters per line into the right range (see LINE LENGTH). The smaller the point size, the larger the page margins will need to be, and vice versa.

FEAR OF WHITE SPACE

"But if I use bigger margins, won't a lot of the page be empty?" Sure. Is that a problem?

The 8.5″ × 11″ paper size is a standard imposed on us by history and tradition. It is arbitrary. It does not represent anyone's idea of a convenient size for good typography.

Here's the proof. Are there any publications that use 8.5″ × 11″ paper? Yes, it's the approximate size of many magazines. But do any of those magazines run text in a single block on the page with one-inch margins? No—never. They use multiple-column layouts or find other ways to divide the page.

So are there any publications that *do* run text in a single block on the page? Sure—books are usually set in a single column. But do you ever see a book printed on 8.5″ × 11″ paper? No—never. It would be too big for comfortable reading.

Professional typographers never use 8.5″ × 11″ paper with a 6.5-inch line length. Neither should you. Set your text according to the principles of good typography. The white space will take care of itself. The pleasure of reading an effectively designed document will soon outweigh the unfamiliarity of extra white space around the edges.

"But with those big margins, I won't get nearly as many words on the page." Let's address that fear with an exercise that brings together some of what you've learned so far.

TYPOGRAPHIC EXERCISE

1. Start a new document in your word processor. Paste in a text of at least 1000 words.

With a 12-point font, "Double" line spacing in Word works out to be 28 points. (If that seems like peculiar math, I agree. See LINE SPACING.) I'm using it here because it's the line-spacing option many people select by default.

(2) Format this new document as follows: page margins of one inch per side, font is TIMES NEW ROMAN, POINT SIZE is 12, LINE SPACING is "Double" (if you're using Word; if not, use exactly 28 points), FIRST-LINE INDENT is half an inch, and no space between paragraphs. I'll call this document A.

(3) Start another new document in your word processor. Paste in the same text.

(4) Format this second document as follows: page margins of two inches per side, font is still Times New Roman, point size is 11, line spacing is exactly 15 points, first-line indent is still half an inch, and still no space between paragraphs. I'll call this document B.

Shortcut: the "before" and "after" samples in RESEARCH MEMOS are pretty close to the formatting of documents A and B.

(5) Print both documents. Which one looks more like a professionally typeset book: A or B?

(6) Which document is more comfortable to read: A or B?

(7) Which document contains more words per page: A or B? Hint: use word count. See LINE LENGTH for instructions.

I'm guessing you answered B to the last three questions. If so, you're seeing how good typography can be a benevolent force—it improves the appearance and legibility of your text with no compromise in words per page.

BY THE WAY

➡ Do margins all have to be the same size? No. To fit more text on the page, reduce the top and bottom margins. Your line length will stay the same, but you'll get more lines per page. To make the text block appear centered vertically, try making the bottom margin about a quarter-inch larger than the top margin. (An old typographer's trick—otherwise, the text block can look like it's sagging.) Finally, there's no rule that a text block has to be centered on the page horizontally. For an asymmetric layout, make the difference between the left and right margins at least one inch—weak asymmetry will just look like a layout error.

➤ The best way to judge a layout is with your eyes, not with a calculator. But typographers have long enjoyed fiddling with layouts that incorporate specific mathematical ratios. Most famous among these is the *golden ratio*, which is approximately 1.618:1. If you set page margins of 2.23 inches on all four sides of 8.5″×11″ paper, the proportions of your text block will be close to the golden ratio.

Please note:
BODY TEXT*
is the most common
element of a document.
Therefore, how the body
text looks will have the
most noticeable effect
on the appearance
of the document.
Consequently,
you should
set up the
body text
FIRST.

Start with
font, POINT SIZE,
LINE SPACING, and
LINE LENGTH, because
those four decisions will
largely determine how
the body text will
look. OK?

body text

Four important considerations

* Meaning, the text that's the main content of your document.

While I'll stop short of calling it a rule, I strongly recommend using a serif font—not a sans serif font—for body text. Most books, newspapers, and magazines use serif fonts for body text. It's the traditional choice and still the best choice.

hyphenation

Mandatory for justified text; optional otherwise

Hyphenation is the automated process of breaking words between lines to create more consistency across a text block.

In JUSTIFIED TEXT, hyphenation is mandatory.

In left-aligned text—

> Hyphenation evens the irregular right edge of the text, called the *rag*. Hyphenation is optional for left-aligned text because the rag will still be somewhat irregular, even with hyphenation. Hyphenation doesn't improve text legibility. Consider turning it off. (This paragraph is left-aligned but not hyphenated.)

> Hyphenation evens the irregular right edge of the text, called the *rag*. Hyphenation is optional for left-aligned text because the rag will still be somewhat irregular, even with hyphenation. Hyphenation doesn't improve text legibility. Consider turning it off. (This paragraph is left-aligned and hyphenated.)

As LINE LENGTH gets shorter, hyphenation becomes essential. Why? With hyphenation off, your word processor can only break lines at word spaces. As the lines get shorter, there are fewer words and hence fewer possible break points, making awkward breaks more likely.

HOW TO TURN HYPHENATION ON (OR OFF)

WORD 2003 | ‹Tools› ➜ ‹Language› ➜ ‹Hyphenation› ➜ *check (or uncheck)* ‹Automatically hyphenate document›

WORD 2007 & 2010 | ‹Page Layout› ➜ ‹Page Setup› *panel* ➜ ‹Hyphenation› ➜ ‹Automatic› *(or* ‹None›*)*

WORDPERFECT | *Select all text.* ‹Tools› ➜ ‹Language› ➜ ‹Hyphenation› ➜ *check (or uncheck)* ‹Turn hyphenation on›

PAGES | *Inspector (command + option + i)* ➜ *document icon (first icon in the top row)* ➜ ‹Document› ➜ *check (or uncheck)* ‹Hyphenate›

Sometimes you may want to suppress automatic hyphenation. For instance, HEADINGS are relatively short, so hyphenation often causes more problems than it solves.

B.   This Court has personal jurisdiction over MegaCorp because its head-
quarters are in San Luis Obispo.   WRONG

B.   This Court has personal
jurisdiction over MegaCorp because
its headquarters are in San Luis Obispo.   RIGHT

Hyphenation can be suppressed in a single paragraph, or a set of paragraphs, if you suppress hyphenation within PARAGRAPH AND CHARACTER STYLES.

HOW TO SUPPRESS HYPHENATION IN A PARAGRAPH

WORD | *Right-click in the text and select* ‹Paragraph› ➜ ‹Line and Page Breaks› ➜ ‹Don't hyphenate›

WORDPERFECT | *Select the paragraph.* ‹Tools› ➜ ‹Language› ➜ ‹Hyphenation› ➜ *uncheck* ‹Turn hyphenation on›

PAGES | *Inspector (command + option + i)* ➜ *T icon in the top row (fourth from left)* ➜ ‹More› ➜ ‹Remove hyphenation for paragraph›

BY THE WAY

➜   You can exert rudimentary control over automatic hyphenation. If you're curious, search your help file for "hyphenation options." Over the years, I've never touched these, so I doubt you'll need to either. The NONBREAKING HYPHEN and the OPTIONAL HYPHEN solve most hyphenation problems, and even those are pretty rare.

block quotations

Don't go on and on

Formatting *block quotations* is not hard. Reduce the POINT SIZE and LINE SPACING slightly. Indent the text block between half an inch and a full inch on the left side, and optionally the same on the right. As with FIRST-LINE INDENTS, make the side indents large enough to be noticed, but not so large that the LINE LENGTH is too short. Don't put quotation marks at the ends—they're redundant.

Block quotations are sometimes unavoidable. If a dispute involves the interpretation of an agreement, accuracy may demand extensive quoting.

But pay attention to length. Lawyers sometimes put voluminous material into a block quotation intending to signal "Hey, I quoted a lot of this source because it's really important!" The actual signal a reader often gets is "Hey, I didn't write any of this, I just cribbed it from somewhere else!" The reader's next thought is usually "Great, I can skip this," or "What does this have to do with this case?"

If you want readers to pay attention to quoted material, edit it carefully and integrate it into the text. Don't just shovel it into a block quotation.

bulleted and numbered lists

Don't type them manually

Are you still making *bulleted and numbered lists* by manually typing bullets or numbers at the beginning of each line?

In the 21st century, no one should be doing this task by hand. Manually formatted lists are a waste of time and prone to error. Use automated lists. I can get you started, but if you're unfamiliar with automated lists, spend some time with your word processor's manual or help file.

HOW TO INSERT AN AUTOMATED LIST

WORD 2003 | ‹Format› → ‹Bullets & Numbering› → ‹Bulleted›, ‹Numbered›, *or* ‹Outline Numbered›

WORD 2007 & 2010 | ‹Home› ➨ ‹Paragraph› *panel. The three buttons in the upper-left corner will start a new list: the first button starts a bulleted list, the second a numbered list, the third an outline list.*

WORDPERFECT | ‹Insert› ➨ ‹Outline/Bullets & Numbering›. *The* ‹Bullets› *tab offers bulleted lists; the* ‹Numbers› *tab offers numbered and outline lists.*

PAGES | *Open the Styles drawer (command + shift + t). If the list styles are not visible, click the list icon in the lower right corner of the Styles drawer. Then choose from* ‹Bullet›, *‹Numbered List›, or* ‹Harvard› *(an outline list).*

BY THE WAY

➨ As I suggested in MIXING FONTS, it's acceptable to set a list index (i.e., a bullet or a number) in a different font than the list item itself. You can also make the list index a smaller POINT SIZE.

➨ Asterisks are sometimes used as bullets, but they're not qualified for the job—they're too small, and they sit too high.

➨ Look out for overlarge bullets. Like FIRST-LINE INDENTS, they should be big enough to be noticeable, but no bigger. I usually prefer hollow bullets to solid bullets because they're more subtle.

➨ A *dingbat* is a nonalphabetic typographic ornament. That's why those symbol fonts on your computer have names like Zapf Dingbats and Wingdings. Dingbat fonts can be a good source of alternative bullets and numbers. Simple geometric dingbats are better than pictorial ones, which don't translate to small sizes. Be aware that these dingbat fonts sometimes contain symbols with cultural or religious significance—tread carefully if the symbol is unfamiliar to you.

➨ Word processors use automatic list detection by default. When you type something that looks like a bulleted or numbered list, it's converted into an automated list. If that method works for you, great. I turn off this feature because I find it only guesses right about half the time.

Advanced rules

tables

The best tool for gridded or complex layouts

The good news: *tables* are one of the handiest tools in your word processor. A table is usually the right solution for layout problems where WHITE-SPACE CHARACTERS aren't up to the task.

The bad news: tables can be difficult to use. The user interface for editing them is complex and finicky. While I can't give you a full tutorial on using tables—refer to your manual or help file—I can give you a few directional tips.

I've already pointed out the ways in which bad typewriter habits have endured (e.g., UNDERLINING, MONOSPACED FONTS). But the unfortunate truth about word processors is that their basic model for page layout is similar to that of a typewriter of a hundred years ago: the document is handled as one big column of text. That's great if all you need is one big column of text. It's not so great otherwise.

These tips about formatting tables apply equally well to spreadsheets.

A table is useful if you have a spreadsheet-style grid of data. In the typewriter era, a grid like this would have been handled with TABS. These days, you'd use a table.

A table is also useful if text in your layout needs to be positioned side-by-side or floating at specific locations on the page. (Two common examples are LETTERHEAD and CAPTION PAGES.) Making these is frustrating with basic layout tools but very easy with tables.

HOW TO INSERT A TABLE

WORD | ‹Insert› ➜ ‹Tables› *panel* ➜ ‹Table› ➜ *drag your cursor around the grid to set the number of rows and columns.*

WORDPERFECT | ‹Table› ➜ ‹Create› ➜ *set the number of rows and columns.*

PAGES | ‹Insert› ➜ ‹Table›. *Pages will give you a four-row, three-column table and open the table editor in the Inspector to allow further adjustments.*

There are many ways to format a table. But your word processor's default tables have two formatting defects you should always fix: *cell borders* and *cell margins*.

Cell borders are the dark lines around each cell in the table. Cell borders are helpful as guides when you're loading information into the table. They're less useful once the table is full. The text in the cells will create an implied grid. Cell borders can make the grid cluttered and difficult to read, especially in tables with many small cells.

	Athos	Porthos	Aramis
Priors?	Yes	No	Yes
Alibi?	No	Yes	Yes
Confession?	No	No	No

CLUTTERED

	Athos	Porthos	Aramis
Priors?	Yes	No	Yes
Alibi?	No	Yes	Yes
Confession?	No	No	No

CLEAN

You could also make this kind of layout using tabs, but a table is the far better choice.

In this example, cell borders are unnecessary. In other cases, they can be useful. The goal is to improve the legibility of the table. When you're ready to format your table, I recommend starting by turning off all the cell borders and then turning them back on as needed. (See RULES AND BORDERS for more tips.)

HOW TO TURN OFF CELL BORDERS

WORD | *Right-click in the table to display menu* ➙ ‹Borders and Shading› ➙ ‹Borders› *tab. In the column on the left labeled* ‹Setting›, *click the button next to* ‹None›. *Click* ‹OK›.

WORDPERFECT | *Right-click in the table to display menu* ➙ ‹Borders / Fill› ➙ ‹Table› *tab. Under* ‹Default cell lines› *is the label* ‹Line› *and a button. Click this button and select the X in the upper left corner. Click* ‹OK›.

PAGES | *If the cursor is inside a cell, click outside the table. Then click the table once to select it. Open the Inspector (command + option + i)* ➙ *table icon in the top row (seventh from left)* ➙ ‹Table›. *Under* ‹Cell Borders› *there's a popup menu to set the cell-border pattern. Change this to* ‹None›.

Cell margins create space between the cell borders and the text of the cell. Increasing the cell margins is the best way to improve the legibility of a dense table.

	Athos	Porthos	Aramis	
Phone	(617) 555-1453	(508) 555-3232	(603) 555-8490	
Cell	(617) 555-3145	(508) 555-2323	(603) 555-8491	
Fax	(617) 555-5413	(508) 555-4545	(603) 555-8492	DENSE

	Athos	Porthos	Aramis	
Phone	(617) 555-1453	(508) 555-3232	(603) 555-8490	
Cell	(617) 555-3145	(508) 555-2323	(603) 555-8491	
Fax	(617) 555-5413	(508) 555-4545	(603) 555-8492	LESS DENSE

The default cell margins, especially in Word, are too tight. With cell margins, a little goes a long way—start around 0.03″ and move in increments of one hundredth of an inch. Also, there's no need to make the cell margins the same on all sides. The top and bottom margins can be bigger than the side margins, if that looks right.

HOW TO SET CELL MARGINS

WORD | *Right-click in the table to display menu* → ‹Table Properties› → ‹Table› *tab* → ‹Options›. *Under* ‹Default cell margins›, *enter the values. You can also use the up and down arrow keys to change the values in increments of 0.01″.*

WORDPERFECT | *Select the whole table. Right-click in the table to display menu* → ‹Format›. *Click the* ‹Column› *tab and adjust left and right cell margins under* ‹Inside margins in column›. *Click the* ‹Row› *tab and adjust top and bottom cell margins under* ‹Row margins›.

PAGES | *If the cursor is inside a cell, click outside the table. Then click the table once to select it. Open the Inspector (command + option + i)* → *T icon in the top row (fourth from left)* → ‹Text› → ‹Inset Margin›. *Use the slider to adjust cell margins. Pages only lets you set one value that applies to all four sides of each cell.*

In traditional printing terminology, a *rule* is a line; a *border* is a box. But in word processors, they're variations of the same function. Rules and borders can be applied to pages, paragraphs, or TABLES.

rules and borders

Use sparingly

Like CENTERED TEXT, BOLD OR ITALIC, and ALL CAPS, rules and borders are best used sparingly. Ask yourself: do you really need a rule or border to make a visual distinction? You can usually get equally good results by increasing the white space around the text. Try that first.

For borders, set the thickness between half a point and one point. Thinner borders can work on professionally printed goods but are

Edward Tufte coined the word **chartjunk** to describe markings that are unnecessary to communicate visual information. Thick grid lines are a common kind of chartjunk.

Tufte's excellent books on information design are included in the BIBLIOGRAPHY.

too fine to reproduce well on an office printer. Thicker borders are counterproductive—they create noise that upstages the information inside. You want to see the data, not the lines around the data.

	Athos	Porthos	Aramis	
Phone	(617) 555-1453	(508) 555-3232	(603) 555-8490	
Cell	(617) 555-3145	(508) 555-2323	(603) 555-8491	
Fax	(617) 555-5413	(508) 555-4545	(603) 555-8492	WRONG

	Athos	Porthos	Aramis	
Phone	(617) 555-1453	(508) 555-3232	(603) 555-8490	
Cell	(617) 555-3145	(508) 555-2323	(603) 555-8491	
Fax	(617) 555-5413	(508) 555-4545	(603) 555-8492	RIGHT

Similarly, don't use patterned borders (i.e., borders made of anything other than a single solid line, like dots, dashes, or double lines). They're unnecessarily complicated.

You have more latitude with rules because they don't accumulate the way borders do. If you want to make a rule thicker than one point or use a pattern, go ahead. But thick or patterned rules still wear out their welcome faster than the classic half-point solid rule.

HOW TO EDIT RULES & BORDERS

WORD 2003 | ‹Format› ➝ ‹Borders and Shading›

WORD 2007 & 2010 | ‹Home› ➝ ‹Paragraph› *panel* ➝ *click the arrow on the right edge of the button that looks like* ▦ *and select* ‹Borders and Shading›

WORDPERFECT | ‹Format› ➝ ‹Paragraph› ➝ ‹Border / Fill›, *or for a table,* ‹Table› ➝ ‹Borders / Fill›

PAGES | *Inspector (command + option + i)* ➝ *T icon in the top row (fourth from left)* ➝ ‹More›. *Use the controls under* ‹Border & Rules›. *For a table, click the table icon in the Inspector and use the controls under* ‹Cell Borders›.

Never make rules and borders out of repeated typographic char-)
acters, like punctuation, HYPHENS AND DASHES, or MATH)
SYMBOLS. Particularly ridiculous is the habit of using stacked pa-)
rentheses to make a vertical line on CAPTION PAGES. Not only is)
it uglier than a vertical rule, it's much harder to assemble. These)
habits have been passed down from typewriters. They're obsolete.)

)

BY THE WAY

➜ If you attach a rule to HEADINGS, try putting it above the heading
(rather than below, which is usually the default). Then the rule is separating the end of the previous section and the current heading, instead of separating the current heading from its own section.

widow and orphan control

Your call

Picture a paragraph that starts at the bottom of one page and continues at the top of the next page. When only the last line of the
paragraph appears at the top of the next page, that line is called a
widow. When only the first line of the paragraph appears at the bottom of the first page, that line is called an *orphan*.

Widow and orphan control prevents both. Orphans are moved to the
next page with the rest of the paragraph. To cure widows, lines are
moved from the bottom of one page to the top of the next. It's a little more complicated than it sounds because curing a widow cannot create a new orphan, nor vice versa.

Be aware that if you use widow and orphan control, you will frequently see blank lines at the bottom of your pages. This is normal,
since lines must be transplanted to cure the problem.

Widow and orphan control in a word processor is all-or-nothing.
You can't control widows and orphans separately, even though widows are more distracting. Why? Orphans appear at the beginning

of a paragraph, so they're at least a full line. But widows can be any length, even a single word, because they appear at the end of a paragraph.

Do you need widow and orphan control? Try it. See how it looks. In my own work, I approach widow and orphan control the same way I approach LIGATURES—I only use it if widows and orphans are causing a visible problem. Otherwise, I find that the blank lines at the bottom of the page are more annoying than the widows and orphans.

HOW TO TURN ON WIDOW & ORPHAN CONTROL

WORD | *Right-click in the text and select* ‹Paragraph› ➙ ‹Line and Page Breaks› ➙ *check* ‹Widow / Orphan control›

WORDPERFECT | ‹Format› ➙ ‹Keep Text Together› ➙ *under* ‹Widow / Orphan›, *check* ‹Prevent the first and last lines of paragraphs from being separated across pages›

PAGES | *Inspector (command + option + i)* ➙ *T icon in the top row (fourth from left)* ➙ ‹More› ➙ *check* ‹Prevent widow & orphan lines›

BY THE WAY

➙ You can also cure isolated widows and orphans with some judicious editing. But don't use a HARD LINE BREAK or CARRIAGE RETURN.

keep lines together

Always use with headings

Keep lines together ensures that all lines in a paragraph appear on the same page. If the last line of the paragraph won't fit on the current page, the whole paragraph gets moved to the next page.

Use this option with HEADINGS to prevent them from starting at the bottom of one page and continuing at the top of the next. That looks bad.

Like WIDOW AND ORPHAN CONTROL, keeping lines together will create gaps at the bottom of pages. But unlike widow and orphan control, you only want to keep lines together in special situations, not as part of your default text formatting.

Why? Keeping lines together is a blunter technique. It only works on whole paragraphs, so the longer the paragraph, the bigger the gap.

If you need to make groups of elements stick together, the keep-lines-together option works well with HARD LINE BREAKS. Recall that hard line breaks don't create a new paragraph, but rather a set of lines. Keeping lines together will ensure this set of lines appears on a single page.

For instance, I like to keep lines together in signature blocks:

May 19, 2013   FALKENBURG, FESTER & FUNK

                                  By:_____
                                  Cadmium Eaglefeather
                                  Attorney for Plaintiff

Here, I've put a hard line break at the end of each line. Then I've set the whole signature block—which is a single paragraph—to keep lines together. That way, I don't have to worry that half the block will end up on one page and half on the next. All of it travels together.

Another example: I once had to prepare a jury-instruction form that required an index of instructions where the judge could enter his rulings:

CACI 204.   Willful suppression of evidence
____ Given as proposed
____ Given as modified
____ Refused
____ Withdrawn

The problem was that the four choices kept getting split up by page breaks. The solution was to put hard line breaks after each choice and keep the lines together to make sure the choices moved as a unit.

HOW TO KEEP LINES TOGETHER

WORD | *Right-click in the text and select* ‹Paragraph› → ‹Line and Page Breaks› → *check* ‹Keep lines together›

WORDPERFECT | ‹Format› → ‹Keep Text Together› → *check* ‹Keep selected text together on same page›

PAGES | *Inspector (command + option + i)* → *T icon in the top row (fourth from left)* → ‹More› → *check* ‹Keep lines together›

keep with next paragraph

Always use with headings

Keep with next paragraph binds the last line of a paragraph to the first line of the next. It ensures no page break happens between the two paragraphs. It's like KEEP LINES TOGETHER, except it works between paragraphs instead of within a paragraph.

Always use this option with HEADINGS. It looks bad if a heading appears at the bottom of a page and the text it's introducing starts on the next page. Keeping with the next paragraph prevents this.

The keep-with-next-paragraph option is a little boring on its own. It gets more interesting when used with its friend, the keep-lines-together option. For instance, let's return to the jury-instruction example:

CACI 204. Willful suppression of evidence
____ Given as proposed
____ Given as modified
____ Refused
____ Withdrawn

Here, the name of the jury instruction is one paragraph, and the four choices below are a second paragraph. The four choices won't get separated from each other because they're glued together with the keep-lines-together option. But we don't want the instruction name getting separated from the choices either. By setting the instruction name to keep with next paragraph, all five lines are guaranteed to move as a unit.

Why didn't I make the whole block one paragraph? So I could apply a separate paragraph style to the names of the instructions, and reformat all of them as a group. (See PARAGRAPH AND CHARACTER STYLES.)

HOW TO KEEP WITH NEXT PARAGRAPH

WORD | *Right-click in the text and select* ‹Paragraph› ➙ ‹Line and Page Breaks› ➙ *check* ‹Keep with next›

WORDPERFECT | *No direct support for keeping with next paragraph. Some say you can approximate the effect with* ‹Format› ➙ ‹Keep Text Together› ➙ ‹Conditional end of page› ➙ *enter the* ‹Number of lines to keep together›. *I'll leave the rest as an exercise for WordPerfect fans.*

PAGES | *Inspector (command + option + i)* ➙ *T icon in the top row (fourth from left)* ➙ ‹More› ➙ *check* ‹Keep with following paragraph›

page break before

Alternative to hard page breaks

Page break before ensures that a paragraph starts at the top of a new page. Visually, there's no difference between using the page-break-before option and typing a HARD PAGE BREAK in front of the paragraph. But that's only efficient for the occasional paragraph.

The page-break-before option is intended to be incorporated into PARAGRAPH AND CHARACTER STYLES so all paragraphs of a particular style will start at the top of a new page. For instance, the top-level headings of a long document—typing hard page breaks in front of each heading would be tedious.

HOW TO USE PAGE BREAK BEFORE

WORD | *Right-click in the text and select* ‹Paragraph› ➜ ‹Line and Page Breaks› ➜ *check* ‹Page break before›

WORDPERFECT | *Not supported. You're stuck using hard page breaks.*

PAGES | *Inspector (command + option + i)* ➜ *T icon in the top row (fourth from left)* ➜ ‹More› ➜ *check* ‹Paragraph starts on a new page›

columns

Your call

They're unusual in legal documents, but I don't object to *columns* in a long document like a contract or a settlement agreement. Columns are an easy way to get a shorter and more legible LINE LENGTH without having to use large margins. On a standard 8.5″× 11″ page, two or three columns are fine; four is too many.

Usually columns look neatest when the rows of text are aligned vertically between columns. Look at a decent newspaper for an example. Getting this result takes a little extra effort. Note your LINE SPACING and make sure any SPACE BETWEEN PARAGRAPHS works out to a whole multiple of the line spacing. The two most common options: set space between paragraphs to zero, or set it to be the same as the line spacing.

A *watermark* is a notice (e.g., "Draft," "Confidential") that's printed in the background of a page. Often in six-inch letters. Diagonally. In red.

Watermarks interact poorly with the text, creating visual noise that distracts from reading. (It's a variation of the problem noted in RULES AND BORDERS.) Also, watermarks can darken considerably when photocopied, aggravating the problem.

It's hard to make watermarks look good. Better to relocate the watermark text somewhere inside the header or footer.

watermarks

Avoid

If you practice in a jurisdiction that requires court filings with *line numbers*, you have faced the vexing problem of keeping the line numbers vertically aligned with the text.

The secret is simple: use exact LINE SPACING with the line numbers and the BODY TEXT.

California state courts require filings to use double line spacing (which works out to 28 lines per page), 12-point type, and line numbers in the left margin. I'll use this as the basic model and you can adapt it to the rules in your jurisdiction.

① Create a new document with one-inch margins.

② In the body of the document, in 12 point, type a paragraph of about five lines that looks like this:

HHHHHHHHHHHHHHHHHHHHHHHHHHHHHH
HHHHHHHHHHHHHHHHHHHHHHHHHHHHHH
HHHHHHHHHHHHHHHHHHHHHHHHHHHHHH
HHHHHHHHHHHHHHHHHHHHHHHHHHHHHH
HHHHHHHHHHHHHHHHHHHHHHHHHHHHHH

line numbers

Exact line spacing is the key

California Rule of Court 2.108(1) also allows filings to use "one and one-half" line spacing, which works out to 37 lines per page. Strangely, I've never seen a 37-line filing. Is it because California lawyers don't know about the rule, or because they don't know how to make a 37-line template? (Follow the instructions here but use 18 points of line spacing instead of 24.)

③ To get true double line spacing, you need to set your line spacing to exactly twice the POINT SIZE. The H paragraph is set in 12 point, so select the whole paragraph and change its line spacing to exactly 24 points. Don't use the "Double" line spacing option in your word processor—despite the name, you'll end up with line spacing larger than you want. (See LINE SPACING.)

④ Open the document header for editing.

WORD 2003 | ‹View› ➡ ‹Header and Footer›

WORD 2007 & 2010 | *In ‹Print Layout› view, double-click near the top of the page.*

WORDPERFECT | *If no header exists, add one. ‹Insert› ➡ ‹Header / Footer›. After adding a header, click in the header box that appears on the page.*

PAGES | *Skip this step. Instead, hold down the command key and click in the corner of the document so there's no active text area.*

⑤ Create a tall, narrow text box in the left margin. (For those unfamiliar, a *text box* lets you put text in an arbitrary position on the page, outside the flow of the main document.)

In Word and WordPerfect, the new text box may have an unwanted border. If so, right-click in the text box and use the menu options to remove the border.

WORD 2003 | ‹Insert› ➡ ‹Text Box›. *Click and drag on the page to create the box.*

WORD 2007 & 2010 | ‹Insert› ➡ ‹Text› *panel* ➡ ‹Text Box› ➡ ‹Draw Text Box›. *Click and drag on the page to create the box.*

WORDPERFECT | ‹Insert› *menu* ➡ ‹Text Box›. *A default text box will appear. Adjust the size and position as needed. Right-click the text box and select ‹Wrap› ➡ ‹Behind Text›.*

PAGES | ‹Insert› ➡ ‹Text Box›. *A default text box will appear. Adjust the size and position as needed. Select the text box and then select ‹Format› ➡ ‹Advanced› ➡ ‹Move Object to Section Master›.*

⑥ In the text box, type your line numbers. Use a HARD LINE BREAK between each number, not a CARRIAGE RETURN, so the whole set of numbers is one paragraph. Select all the numbers. As you did before, use paragraph formatting to set the line spacing to exactly 24 points.

⑦ Drag the text box near the H paragraph so it looks approximately aligned.

⑧ Zoom in closely to the top left corner of the H paragraph so you can see the H paragraph on the right, and the first few numbers in the text box on the left. Select the text box and use the arrows on your keyboard to move the text box vertically until the bottoms of the numbers line up with the bottoms of the lines in the H paragraph.

That's it. You should now have line numbers that repeat on every page and that line up with the BODY TEXT. Remember—all the paragraphs in your document, including headings, must have line spacing of exactly 24 points and no SPACE BETWEEN PARAGRAPHS. Otherwise, the text will no longer align with the line numbers.

BY THE WAY

➤ The line numbers themselves don't have to be the same POINT SIZE or font style as the BODY TEXT. I like to make them smaller so they look more like a background element on the page. (See MAXIMS OF PAGE LAYOUT for the idea of contrasting foregrounds and backgrounds.) Make these adjustments to the line numbers before aligning them with the body text.

➤ See the CAPTION PAGE and MOTION sample documents for more tips on typography in court filings.

Bates numbering

Try orange Franklin Gothic

Just as paper is yielding to PDF as the preferred format for discovery, manually stamped *Bates numbering* is yielding to digital numbering.

I prefer the convenience of digital Bates numbering. But I miss the look of the stamp. The blue ink and the distinct font made the number easy to spot on the page, even after being photocopied. Digital Bates numbering is often small, black, and set in TIMES NEW ROMAN or Arial—all of which camouflages the numbers.

Tips for making digital Bates numbers stand out:

1. Make the POINT SIZE reasonably big—not smaller than 12 point.

2. Use a font with good numerals. I like Franklin Gothic Medium or Franklin Gothic Demi. Avoid fonts that are condensed or dark on the page (e.g., Arial Black). These fonts are hard to read at small sizes and don't stand up well to scanning or photocopying.

3. Use color. I use a medium-dark orange. Not the most attractive, but it stands out because orange rarely occurs in discovery (unless you're suing a carrot company). Orange isn't so bright that it gets washed out when reproduced in black and white.

4. Make sure your Bates numbers don't get stamped in the content of the document. Adobe Acrobat can shrink documents uniformly so there's a clean margin for the numbering.

HOW TO APPLY CUSTOMIZED BATES NUMBERING

ADOBE ACROBAT | ‹Advanced› → ‹Document Processing› → ‹Bates Numbering› → ‹Add›. *Select the documents to be numbered and click ‹OK›. You'll be taken to the Acrobat ‹Add Header and Footer› window.*

The middle of this window has six boxes corresponding to locations on the page (‹Left Header Text›, ‹Center Header Text›, and so on). Click in the box where you want your Bates number. Click ‹Insert Bates Number› and then click ‹OK›. You will get a dinky, illegible Bates number.

Near the top of the window, under the label ‹Font›, change the font and the point size. Click the black square to the right to change the color.

To ensure your Bates numbers don't collide with any page content, click ‹Appearance Options› and check ‹Shrink document to avoid overwriting the document's text and graphics›. Click ‹OK›.

Make any other necessary adjustments in the main window. Click ‹OK› to apply the Bates numbering.

Implementing good typography is often a chore and a bore. For everyone, not just for lawyers. *Paragraph and character styles* eliminate most of the drudgery.

Styles are the DNA of document layout. Styles make it easy to control typography across a single document. They also let you make templates that can be reused across multiple documents. The result is better, more consistent typography in every document with less work per document.

I find it curious that so many lawyers don't know how to use styles. They format their documents the old-fashioned way: word by word and paragraph by paragraph.

Do you check your spelling by having a human being read your draft? No, you use an automated spelling checker. Do you copy a document by putting each page on the photocopier glass? No, you put the whole thing in the sheet feeder.

If you plan to have a long-term relationship with good typography, I recommend you learn how to use styles too.

paragraph and character styles

The secret to typographic success

WHY YOU SHOULD CARE ABOUT STYLES

Word, WordPerfect, and Pages all offer paragraph and character styles. They work basically the same way, but the details are quite different between the three.

I can't give you a detailed tutorial on using paragraph and character styles. You'll need to spend some time with your manual or help file.

If self-study is too daunting, consider software training. Training is a great investment. Your word processor is a tool you use every day. If you don't know how to use its most powerful features, you're wasting time every day.

① Styles let you *define sets of formatting attributes* that get applied together. So instead of selecting a heading, changing it to 13 point, bold, and all caps, you can define a style that includes these three attributes, and apply the style to the heading.

What's the benefit? When you come across the next heading, you don't need to individually apply those three attributes. You apply the style you defined before. The headings will then match.

② Styles let you *change formatting* across a class of related elements. Suppose you want to change your headings from 13 point to 13.5 point. Instead of selecting each heading separately and changing the point size—a tedious project—you can change the point size in the heading style definition from 13 point to 13.5 point. Headings using that style will be automatically updated.

What's the benefit? Updating the formatting is centralized and automatic. You can experiment with formatting and layout ideas with little manual effort.

③ Styles can *inherit formatting* from other styles. A change to the parent style will propagate to all the substyles. But a change to the substyle will only affect that one style.

What's the benefit? Inheritance adds another layer of centralized automation—it's like having styles of styles. You can define a set of foundation styles and use them as the basis for more elaborate styles.

HOW TO USE STYLES EFFECTIVELY

Character styles can incorporate attributes of words and sentences, like font, POINT SIZE, LETTERSPACING, BOLD OR ITALIC, ALL CAPS, and SMALL CAPS.

Paragraph styles can incorporate those attributes and also layout attributes like LINE SPACING, FIRST-LINE INDENTS, and RULES AND BORDERS.

Why have two kinds of styles? You can only apply one paragraph style to each paragraph, but you can apply multiple character styles to text within the paragraph.

As a rule of thumb, any time you have two document elements that should be formatted identically, you'll want to use a style.

Initially, you may be inclined to define styles like "Caslon Bold 11.5 point." That's better than applying the same formatting manually. But it overlooks another benefit of styles, which is to define formatting in terms of what each paragraph is used for, rather than how it looks. If you're creating a style for a block quotation, the name "Caslon Bold 11.5 point" is not as good as "Block Quotation." And later, if you change the formatting, the name will still be accurate.

Word processors come with a long list of built-in styles. Word, for instance, has ‹Heading 1› through ‹Heading 9›, ‹Quote›, ‹Caption›, ‹Header›, ‹Footer›, and so on. Many of these styles are wired into other functions. It's good practice to modify the built-in styles when possible rather than create new ones.

When you do this, you'll also notice that many built-in styles are horribly ugly. For example, Word's ‹Header 1› is 14-point blue Cambria, a style with no redeeming qualities. I'm not worried that you'd use it without fixing it first. At this point, you know better.

Successful typography requires you to pay attention to the whole, not just the parts. These maxims summarize the key principles I keep in mind when I'm laying out a document.

① **Decide first how the body text will look.**
Why? Because there's more BODY TEXT than anything else. Four decisions—POINT SIZE, LINE LENGTH, LINE SPACING, and font—largely determine the appearance of the body text. Therefore, these decisions have the biggest influence on the legibility of the text and the overall appearance of the document.

② **Divide the page into foreground and background.**
The foreground contains the most important page elements. (Hint: the body text is usually one of them.) The background contains everything else. Don't let the background elements upstage the foreground elements. And remember that you have a limited number of tools for making distinctions: position, size, font, and sometimes color. (See LETTERHEAD for an example of how to handle the foreground–background relationship.)

③ **Make adjustments with the smallest visible increments.**
Typography thrives on fine details. The difference between not enough and too much can be small.

④ **When in doubt, try it both ways.**
Don't try to resolve typographic decisions with logic. There's no substitute for printing samples of two options and getting a visual reaction.

⑤ **Be consistent.**
Typography quietly describes to readers a structure and hierarchy. Things that are the same should look the same. Things that look different should actually be different. Without

consistent treatment of similar elements, the document will feel random and meandering.

6 **Relate each new element to existing elements.**
The only time you have unfettered discretion is when the page is blank. After that, the page is like a jigsaw puzzle that becomes more constrained with each new piece.

7 **Keep it simple.**
A principle as true in typography as anything else. If you think you need three colors and five fonts, think again.

8 **Imitate what you like.**
Why reinvent the wheel? If you see typography you like—in a book, in a magazine, on a sign—emulate it. Learning to see what's good about other examples of typography makes it easier to solve problems in your own layouts.

9 **Don't fear white space.**
A lot of mediocre typography results from a perceived need to fill space. Things get too big or spread out. Work outward from the text, not inward from the page edges. If the text looks good, the white space will take care of itself.

LETTER FROM
HON. B. F. HALLETT,

TO THE PRESIDENT OF THE MEETING IN FANEUIL HALL,

IN SUPPORT OF THE

NEW CONSTITUTION!

17 LOUISBURG SQUARE, Oct. 11, 1853.

SIR :—The death of a near and valued relative, this morning, has taken from me the power to address my fellow-citizens as I intended to have done this evening, in support of the provisions of the new Constitution. The election of a Governor is a temporary affair. The adoption of the new Constitution will be a great work of democratic progress for a generation. The amendments offered to the people are eminently democratic. They embody the progress of democratic reforms through a struggle of *seventy-three years* in the constitutional history of the Commonwealth!

I am pained to see any intimation that a single Democrat will vote against the new Constitution as a whole. What if it is not all he wanted? Let him reflect how much *more* it is of PROGRESS in popular government than *seven generations* have achieved hitherto, dating from the Old Bay State settlement. Let him reflect, that *if for lack of democratic votes* this new Constitution is lost, the "State Reforms" that he and all of us have inscribed on our banners and contended for for twenty years, will be indefinitely postponed to another and another generation.

It is said that this new Constitution will help the coalition. I deny it. I watched or trod every step of its progress, and I think I know what democratic principles of government are. I speak not as a *partisan* Democrat, but as a democrat in government ; AND I SAY THAT EVERY ESSENTIAL AMENDMENT IN THE NEW CONSTITUTION IS SOUNDLY DEMOCRATIC, and can promote NOTHING but sound democratic good government.

ADOPT this new Constitution, and you abolish all property tests and extend FREE SUFFRAGE TO FIFTY THOUSAND CITIZENS, who are men deprived of the *first* right belonging to man in community, because they cannot purchase it with a tax !

ADOPT this Constitution, and you render inviolate the INDEPENDENCE OF THE BALLOT. You preserve the TOWN DEMOCRACIES by preserving town representation AGAINST CONSOLIDATED AND ABSORBING CITY AND CORPORATION REPRESENTATIVES. You equalize agriculture and commerce, the country and city, by Districting Large Places, and preventing the control of masses of representatives by one party, through the general ticket system. You will give to the people the choice of seventeen classes of officers now under executive patronage. You secure the peoples' right to make and amend their own Constitutions. You can re-establish the inestimable RIGHT OF TRIAL BY JURY. You ingraft in the Constitution a perfect militia code. You can make the judiciary dependent on the SOVEREIGNTY OF THE PEOPLE, with sufficient guards for its independence if honest, and checks for its punishment if corrupt. You substitute general laws for special legislation. But I may not enlarge upon these topics. It would carry me through the speech I had prepared for this evening in vindication of the new Constitution, and which I hope to present to my fellow-citizens at some other time, should they desire it.

No question of State concern has come up in Massachusetts for forty years which so well deserved every democratic vote in the State, as does the new Constitution. I know that whereof I speak, for I have studied it. NO DEMOCRAT WHO STUDIES THESE AMENDMENTS CAN VOTE AGAINST THEM.

In conclusion, let me remind those with whom I love to act politically, that in 1845 the Whig State Address charges the Democrats with "a *criminal* design to change the Constitution of the Commonwealth." The Democrats in their Address replied, "*we are ready for reform, whenever and wherever the people demand it.*"

Let this be our answer now, and LET EVERY DEMOCRAT take it with him to the polls, and deposit his YEA for the entire new Constitution !

Very respectfully your fellow-citizen,

B. F. HALLETT.

ABOVE That's what I call a letter. Published in Boston, 1853.

Sample documents

NOW IT'S TIME TO PUT EVERYTHING together. Like good writing, good typography isn't determined by elements in isolation, but by the relationship of those elements and the effect of the whole.

So far we've looked at typographic rules individually. In this chapter, we'll look at these rules in the context of some common documents. Your goal is to get better at seeing typographic flaws in layouts and fixing them.

Each sample document is presented in the form of a before-and-after demonstration: "before" represents a typical layout with the usual bad habits; "after" represents a layout upgraded with the lessons of this book.

All the samples in this chapter were created with good old Microsoft Word 2007—no special trickery was used. The names and situations in the sample documents are, of course, fictitious.

You can download PDF versions of these sample documents from the web if you want to study them more carefully. Go to `http://typographyforlawyers.com/code/` and enter the numerical code listed beneath the sample.

caption pages

Use a table for best results

If this book were a law-school class, reformatting a caption page could be the final exam. Caption pages pack a lot of typographic issues into a small area. How many can you spot?

BEFORE

① MONOSPACED FONT.
Too much text in ALL CAPS.
No LETTERSPACING of caps.

② Unnecessary UNDERLINING.
LINE SPACING too tight.
RULES AND BORDERS made out of punctuation.

③ Vertical rules too thick.
FIRST-LINE INDENT is too large.
LINE NUMBERS don't align with BODY TEXT.
Inconsistent capitalization in HEADING.
Awkward line break in heading.

Despite its appearance, this example did not come from 1957. It's a nearly exact replica of a document filed in 2010 by the U.S. government in a criminal case I was working on. The names, of course, have been changed.

The best way to lay out a caption page is with a TABLE. At minimum, the party names and title should go in a two-column table, like so:

Party names	Title

You can also start the table at the top of the page and put the attorneys and court name in it too. That's how I prefer to do it—the table makes it easy to adjust the position of each element. To make cells spanning two columns, add new rows and then merge the cells in each row.

Attorney names	
Court name	
Party names	Title

The text at the bottom of the page starts outside the table.

```
1   GEORGE CRUIKSHANK
    United States Attorney
2   LAURENCE STERNE                              ①
    Assistant United States Attorney
3   312 North Spring Street
    Los Angeles, California 90012
4   Telephone: (213) 555-3547
    Facsimile: (213) 555-3713
5   E-mail: laurence.sterne@usdoj.gov

6   Attorneys for Plaintiff
    United States of America
7

8

9                   UNITED STATES DISTRICT COURT

10           FOR THE CENTRAL DISTRICT OF CALIFORNIA

11
    UNITED STATES OF AMERICA,      )   Case No. _____
12                                 )
                    Plaintiff;     )   GOVERNMENT'S NOTICE OF REQUEST
13                                 )   FOR DETENTION
         v.                        )
14                                 )
    TRISTRAM SHANDY,               )
15                                 )                  ②
                    Defendant.     )
16                                 )
    ----------------------------------
17

18

19
            Plaintiff, United States of America, by and through its
20
    counsel of record, hereby requests detention of defendant and gives
21
    notice of the following material factors:
22
    _____   1.  Temporary 10-day Detention Requested (§ 3142(d)) on the
23
                 following grounds:
24
         ③      a.    present offense committed while defendant was on
25
                      release pending (felony trial), (sentencing),
26
                      (appeal), or on (probation) (parole).
27

28
```

Code 17301

Call me a scofflaw, but I don't align the text in the top half of the page to the line numbers. It's possible, but it takes a lot of fiddling and often results in less legible text.

AFTER

① Monospaced font replaced with Stempel Garamond.
All caps replaced with bold, or nothing. (SMALL CAPS would be another option.)
Address lines separated with HARD LINE BREAKS.
Letterspacing added to court name.

② Underlining removed.
Line spacing looser in top half of page.
Rules and borders made with table-cell borders.
POINT SIZE of party names and title slightly bigger than other text.

③ First-line indent reduced.
Line numbers align with body text.
Capitalization in heading fixed.
Hard line break inserted in heading before "on."

In the address block, notice that surplus words (e.g., "Telephone," "E-mail") have been deleted. Cutting unnecessary words will always make your text easier to read. This is especially true when you need to fit a lot of data in a small space. (See also BUSINESS CARDS.)

Recall the second MAXIM OF PAGE LAYOUT—*divide the page into foreground and background*. The vertical rules on a caption page should seem like part of the background—they should not be darker or more prominent than the body text in the foreground. Removing unnecessary rules will make the body text area feel less cramped. I use as few as possible. In this revised version, I removed the vertical rule on the right and one on the left. I made the remaining rule thinner and moved it away from the text.

Court filings have ugly typography as a matter of habit, not requirement. Court rules can be strict, but there's still plenty of room for good typography (see HOW TO INTERPRET COURT RULES).

1	George Cruikshank, United States Attorney
2	Laurence Sterne, Assistant United States Attorney
	312 North Spring Street
3	Los Angeles, CA 90012
4	(213) 555-3547
	(213) 555-3713 fax
5	laurence.sterne@usdoj.gov
6	
	Attorneys for Plaintiff
7	United States of America
8	

①

UNITED STATES DISTRICT COURT

FOR THE CENTRAL DISTRICT OF CALIFORNIA

12	**United States of America,**	Case No. _____
13		
14	Plaintiff;	
	v.	**Government's Notice of**
15		**Request for Detention**
16	**Tristram Shandy,**	
17	Defendant.	②
18		

19

20   Plaintiff, United States of America, by and through its counsel of record,

21 hereby requests detention of defendant and gives notice of the following material

22 factors:

23   _____ 1.   **Temporary 10-day detention requested (§ 3142(d))**

24   **on the following grounds:**

25   a.   present offense committed while defendant was on release

26   pending (felony trial), (sentencing), (appeal), or on

27 ③   (probation) (parole).

28

motions

*Extra attention
to legibility is
time well spent*

As a litigator, I understand that motions are often written under deadline pressure that make good typography seem like an unaffordable luxury.

But when is it more important to have your reader's full attention? You're asking a judge to order a remedy—or, if you're opposing, to refrain from ordering that remedy. The issue is important enough to have reached the judge's desk. The ruling may not be appealable. Shouldn't you put your best foot forward?

"Yes, but where do I find the time?" You think about typography *before* you write your motion—by setting up a motion template with PARAGRAPH AND CHARACTER STYLES that handle most of the typography chores as you write. When you get to the end, there's not much left to do.

Or you can submit motions that look like they just rolled out of bed.

BEFORE

(1) Top level of HEADINGS wasted with section label.
No LETTERSPACING in all-caps heading.
UNDERLINING throughout.
Arial used for body text and headings.
Word by word capitalization of subheadings.
Two spaces between sentences.
No HYPHENATION in JUSTIFIED TEXT.

(2) LINE LENGTH too wide and text too close to vertical rules.
LINE NUMBERS and BODY TEXT misaligned.
Headings are not substantive.

(3) Last heading breaks onto next page.
Hyphens used next to page number instead of dashes.
POINT SIZE of footer is too large.
No letterspacing in footer text.

1   Plaintiff Julius Caesar submits the following memorandum in support of his motion to

2   compel production of financial records.

3   **I.   MEMORANDUM OF POINTS AND AUTHORITIES**

4   **A.   Background Facts And Procedural History**

5   Previously, the Court denied the Defendants' motion for summary adjudication of

6   Caesar's claims for punitive damages. (<u>Brutus Decl</u>. ¶ 1.) Caesar served the Defendants

7   with timely notices to produce financial records at trial. (<u>Brutus Decl</u>. ¶ 2.) The Defendants

8   responded with boilerplate objections to Caesar's requests.   None of the Defendants

9   produced any financial records. (<u>Brutus Decl</u>. ¶ 3.)

10   This motion seeks to compel the Defendants to produce these records, and pay

11   sanctions to Caesar of $1000.

12   **B.   Caesar Wants The Financial Records**

13   Because this is a punitive damages case, Caesar is entitled to subpoena documents

14   "to be available at the trial for the purpose of establishing the profits or financial condition" of

15   the Defendants. <u>Cal. Civ. Code</u> § 3295(c).

16   Caesar has a right to these records even without showing that there is a "substantial

17   probability that [he] will prevail." <u>Id</u>. That's the rule for pretrial discovery of financial records,

18   but not for records to be brought to trial. <u>Id</u>.

19   **C.   The Financial Records Are Important**

20   If the jury finds any of the Defendants liable for punitive damages, the jury may then

21   consider "[e]vidence of profit and financial condition" of those defendants to determine the

22   amount of punitive damages. <u>Cal. Civ. Code</u> §§ 3294(a), 3295(d).

23   Furthermore, the Defendants were ordered to stand trial on punitive damages.

24   (<u>Brutus Decl</u>. ¶ 4.) If the jury returns an initial verdict for punitive damages, Caesar will need

25   these financial records to prove the amount of punitive damages.

26   The Defendants cannot circumvent the trial by withholding evidence that the jury must

27   consider. <u>Cal. Civ. Code</u> § 3295(d).

28   **D.   Caesar Will Be Prejudiced Without The Financial Records, So There Is**

-- 2 --

PLAINTIFF'S MOTION TO COMPEL FINANCIAL RECORDS

Code 17701

AFTER

① Letterspacing added to section label.
Underlining removed.
Arial replaced with Goudy Old Style.
Subheadings promoted to main headings. Capitalization corrected.
One space between sentences.
Text is justified and hyphenated.

② Line length narrowed; text farther from vertical rules.
Line numbers aligned with body text.
Headings rewritten to be substantive.

③ Em dashes used next to page number.
Footer point size reduced.
Letterspacing added to footer.
Last heading moved to next page using KEEP LINES TOGETHER.

Notice how much white space has been added around the edges of the text and near the headings. Remember the ninth MAXIM OF PAGE LAYOUT—*don't fear white space.* You needn't fill up every square inch permitted by law. Yes, adding white space will lengthen the document slightly, because you're using less space per page. The benefit is better typography and better legibility. (If you genuinely prefer the motion on the previous page, it's time to pass this book along to a friend.)

POINTS AND AUTHORITIES

Previously, the Court denied the Defendants' motion for summary adjudication of Caesar's claims for punitive damages. (Brutus Decl. ¶ 1.) Caesar served the Defendants with timely notices to produce financial records at trial. (Brutus Decl. ¶ 2.) The Defendants responded with boilerplate objections. None of the Defendants produced any financial records. (Brutus Decl. ¶ 3.) This motion seeks to compel the Defendants to produce these records, and pay sanctions to Caesar of $1000.

1.   Caesar is entitled to the financial records under Civil Code § 3295.

Because this is a punitive damages case, Caesar is entitled to subpoena documents "to be available at the trial for the purpose of establishing the profits or financial condition" of the Defendants. Cal. Civ. Code § 3295(c).

Caesar has a right to these records even without showing that there is a "substantial probability that [he] will prevail." *Id.* That's the rule for pretrial discovery of financial records, but not for records to be brought to trial. *Id.*

2.   Caesar needs the financial records because they are evidence of the Defendants' financial condition and relevant to the second phase of trial.

If the jury finds any of the Defendants liable for punitive damages, the jury may then consider "[e]vidence of profit and financial condition" of those defendants to determine the amount of punitive damages. Cal. Civ. Code §§ 3294(a), 3295(d).

Furthermore, the Defendants were ordered to stand trial on punitive damages. (Brutus Decl. ¶ 4.) If the jury returns an initial verdict for punitive damages, Caesar will need these financial records to prove the amount of punitive damages. The Defendants cannot circumvent the trial by withholding evidence that the jury must consider. Cal. Civ. Code § 3295(d).

– 2 –

PLAINTIFF'S MOTION TO COMPEL FINANCIAL RECORDS

Code 17901

research memos

Bigger margins, smaller point size, tighter line spacing

The problems that afflict research memos also afflict other long documents like settlement agreements and contracts. You can adapt this recipe for any of them.

My legal-writing teacher in law school required memos to be formatted in what I would call the classic typewriter layout—one-inch margins on all sides, 12-point font, and double-spaced lines. Because of its genesis in typewritten documents, this format is the basis of many institutional document-layout rules. For instance, most courts require filings to be in some variation of this format.

But have you ever seen a book, newspaper, or magazine that uses this layout? No. Why not? Because it's not optimally legible. So why would anyone use it? Because it suits the severely limited capabilities of the typewriter. So if we don't use typewriters anymore, why does everyone still use this layout?

My thoughts exactly.

BEFORE

1. PAGE MARGINS too small.
   LINE LENGTH too wide.
   POINT SIZE too big.
   Two spaces between sentences.
   FIRST-LINE INDENTS too deep.
   LINE SPACING too tall.
   JUSTIFIED TEXT without HYPHENATION.

2. UNDERLINING in heading.
   Headings don't align horizontally with paragraphs.

3. Hyphens missing from phrasal adjectives.
   Hyphen used instead of en dash in citation.

Transplanting this document from the 1890s into the present is simple surgery.

To: Cadmium Q. Eaglefeather

From: Trixie Argon

Date: 10 September 2010

Re: Elements of malicious prosecution

①

Malicious prosecution has three elements that must be pleaded and proven: 1) the defendant commenced a judicial proceeding against the plaintiff; 2) the original proceeding was "initiated with malice" and "without probable cause"; and 3) the proceeding was "pursued to a legal termination in [the plaintiff's] favor." *Bertero v. National General Corp.*, 13 Cal. 3d 43, 50 (1974).

A.   Commencement of judicial proceeding   ②

Any civil proceeding where the plaintiff seeks affirmative relief may be the basis of a malicious prosecution claim. The original plaintiff does not need to personally sign the complaint; if he is "actively instrumental" or the "proximate and efficient cause" of the action, he may be liable. *Jacques Interiors v. Petrak*, 188 Cal. App. 3d 1363, 1372 (1987).

B.   Initiated without probable cause and with malice

The malicious prosecution plaintiff must establish both malice and lack of probable cause by the defendant in the underlying action.

③

In a malicious prosecution action against an attorney in a civil suit, the standard for probable cause is whether a reasonable attorney would have thought the underlying claim was tenable at the time the original complaint was filed. See *Sheldon Appel Co. v. Albert & Oliker*, 47 Cal. 3d 863, 885-86 (1989). An attorney may be liable for continuing to prosecute a claim after she discovers the action lacks probable cause, even if there was probable cause at the outset. See *Zamos v. Stroud*, 32 Cal. 4th 958, 970 (2004).

1

AFTER

① Page margins larger (2″ on sides and 1.5″ on top and bottom).
Point size smaller.
One space between sentences.
First-line indents reduced.
Line spacing reduced.
Hyphenation turned on.

② Line length shorter (about 65 characters per line).
No underlining.
Headings align with paragraphs.
Headings half a point larger than body text.
Space added before and after headings.

③ Hyphens added to phrasal adjectives.
En dash in citation.

An additional virtue: the revised layout fits more text on the page.

Note the combination of right-aligned and left-aligned TABS in the first four lines, so all eight pieces of text look like they're positioned against an invisible rectangle. If you have time for them, subtle details make a difference.

SHARING DRAFT DOCUMENTS

If you're working on documents with other lawyers, you have less typographic control and should adjust accordingly.

The major problem is font choice. If you pick a font your collaborator doesn't have, your collaborator won't see the formatting accurately.

This is one of the few situations where SYSTEM FONTS are your best choice. Your collaborators are likely to have them, and these fonts look good on screen, where much of the collaboration happens. If you like, you can reformat with a different font at the end.

Even with system fonts, perfect visual fidelity is not guaranteed. This is one reason some lawyers, me included, like to use numbered paragraphs when working on documents with other lawyers—it provides an unambiguous reference system.

If it's critical that your document appear the same way on your collaborator's screen as it does on yours, the only foolproof technique is to share PDF files and use commenting and review tools on the PDF.

To: Cadmium Q. Eaglefeather
From: Trixie Argon
Date: 10 September 2010
Re: **Elements of malicious prosecution**

Malicious prosecution has three elements that must be pleaded and proven: 1) the defendant commenced a judicial proceeding against the plaintiff; 2) the original proceeding was "initiated with malice" and "without probable cause"; and 3) the proceeding was "pursued to a legal termination in [the plaintiff's] favor." *Bertero v. National General Corp.*, 13 Cal. 3d 43, 50 (1974).

A.   Commencement of judicial proceeding

Any civil proceeding where the plaintiff seeks affirmative relief may be the basis of a malicious-prosecution claim. The original plaintiff does not need to personally sign the complaint; if he is "actively instrumental" or the "proximate and efficient cause" of the action, he may be liable. *Jacques Interiors v. Petrak*, 188 Cal. App. 3d 1363, 1372 (1987).

B.   Initiated without probable cause and with malice

The malicious-prosecution plaintiff must establish both malice and lack of probable cause by the defendant in the underlying action.

In a malicious-prosecution action against an attorney in a civil suit, the standard for probable cause is whether a reasonable attorney would have thought the underlying claim was tenable at the time the original complaint was filed. See *Sheldon Appel Co. v. Albert & Oliker*, 47 Cal. 3d 863, 885–86 (1989). An attorney may be liable for continuing to prosecute a claim after she discovers the action lacks probable cause, even if there was probable cause at the outset. See *Zamos v. Stroud*, 32 Cal. 4th 958, 970 (2004).

The adequacy of an attorney's research is not relevant, because probable cause relies on an objective standard of reasonableness. But if the court finds no probable cause, the thoroughness of the attorney's research may apply to showing malice. See *Sheldon Appel Co.*, 47 Cal. 3d at 875.

The showing of malice requires evidence of "ill will or some improper purpose," ranging "anywhere from open hostility to in-

1 of 3

Code 18301

letterhead

Foreground in front, background in back

Not everything in a page layout is equally important. As I mentioned in MAXIMS OF PAGE LAYOUT, I think of documents as having a foreground, containing the most important elements, and a background, containing everything else. Typography communicates this distinction to the reader visually.

Picture a sheet of letterhead. What's in the foreground? If you said "the address block," then I'm guessing you pictured a blank sheet of letterhead. But letterhead is never used blank. So more accurately, the foreground contains the text of the letter. The background contains the address block.

Yet lawyer letterhead often suffers from two problems. First, the address block (the background) dominates the page, upstaging the text of the letter (the foreground). Second, the foreground and background don't relate to each other visually.

BEFORE

1. Too much space wasted in top margin.
   Too much CENTERED TEXT.
   Long name set in a wide font.
   Redundant and unnecessary words.
   Address block dense and hard to read.
   Address block too large compared to body text.

2. Second office address and date positioned arbitrarily.
   LINE LENGTH too wide.
   Left and right PAGE MARGINS too small.
   FIRST-LINE INDENTS used with SPACE BETWEEN PARAGRAPHS.

3. Signature block positioned arbitrarily.

This letterhead can be improved by making the text of the letter more prominent, reducing the weight of the address block, and making the overall layout less disjointed.

THE LAW OFFICES OF

CADMIUM Q. EAGLEFEATHER, PLC

A PROFESSIONAL LAW CORPORATION
5419 HOLLYWOOD BOULEVARD, SUITE C731
LOS ANGELES, CALIFORNIA 90027
TELEPHONE: (323) 555-1435
FACSIMILE: (323) 555-1439
E-MAIL: CADMIUM@CQELAW.COM

(1)

HAWAII OFFICE

12985 BALDWIN DRIVE
SUITE B22
MAKAWAO, HAWAII 96768
TELEPHONE: (808) 555-5435
FACSIMILE: (808) 555-5439

January 15, 2010

George Falkenburg   (2)
Falkenburg, Fester, and Funk LLP
1252 W. 83rd Street
New York, NY 10012

   Re: *Nicholson v. Amygdala Inc.,* **Case No. B718590125-2**

Dear Mr. Falkenburg:

   In response to your recent request, enclosed is a DVD of photographs I took during the inspection of the Amygdala facility on October 30, 2009.

   I apologize for the delay, but I was recently hospitalized for a concussion sustained while rollerblading. Rest assured that I am on the mend.

   If you have any questions regarding this DVD, please let me know.

                    Sincerely,

(3)   *Cadmium Eaglefeather*

                    CADMIUM Q. EAGLEFEATHER

CQE / bqe
Enclosure

Code 18501

Setting the address block in gray or another color would also help keep it part of the background.

(1) Top margin smaller.
No more centered text.
Unnecessary words removed.
Address block set in lighter, more legible font.
Horizontal rule same width as text of letter.

(2) Address lines separated with HARD LINE BREAKS.
Letter paragraphs align to left side.
Letter starts higher on the page.
Line length narrower; left and right page margins larger.
First-line indents removed.

(3) Second office address used as footer.

The address block at the top is set up with a TABLE:

Name, etc.	
Address	Phone, fax, e-mail

Notice how the horizontal rules in the header and footer define a rectangle that all the page elements relate to in some way, improving the overall cohesion of the layout.

PRODUCTION TIPS FOR LETTERHEAD

The finest letterhead comes from *letterpress printers*, who use old-fashioned metal type. Every major city supports at least a couple of letterpress printers. Most of their business comes from wedding invitations and stationery. It's more expensive than other methods, but the results are nonpareil.

Next up are *offset printers.* (*Offset* is short for *offset lithography*, the process used to make 99% of printed goods.) Offset printers range from high-end commercial outfits to tiny neighborhood shops. I'd like to assure you that price and quality correlate, but they don't. I've worked with neighborhood shops that have done a great job,

The Law Offices of

CADMIUM Q. EAGLEFEATHER

A Professional Law Corporation

5419 Hollywood Boulevard, Suite C731
Los Angeles, CA 90027

(323) 555-1435
(323) 555-1439 fax
cadmium@cqelaw.com

January 15, 2010

George Falkenburg
Falkenburg, Fester, and Funk LLP
1252 W. 83rd Street
New York, NY 10012

Re: *Nicholson v. Amygdala Inc.*, Case No. B718590125-2 ②

Dear Mr. Falkenburg:

In response to your recent request, enclosed is a DVD of photographs
I took during the inspection of the Amygdala facility on October 30,
2009.

I apologize for the delay, but I was recently hospitalized for a concussion sustained while rollerblading. Rest assured that I am on the
mend.

If you have any questions regarding this DVD, please let me know.

Sincerely,

CADMIUM Q. EAGLEFEATHER

CQE / bqe
Enclosure ③

Hawaii Office   12985 Baldwin Drive, Suite B22   Makawao, HI   96768
(808) 555-5435   (808) 555-5439 fax

Code 18701

and big printers that have seriously goofed. Ask a colleague to recommend a printer. If the work isn't right, ask to have it reprinted.

Many offset printers offer graphic-design services as a convenience to their customers, much the same way that bowling alleys rent shoes. These design services are usually fine unless you want the finished work to contain more than a modicum of originality or finesse. In that case, hire an independent graphic designer. (More on that below.)

What about Internet offset printers? (Meaning, websites where you upload a PDF, which is then printed and shipped back to you in a week or so.) I've been pleasantly surprised by the quality of their work. I can recommend them for jobs where you need a small print run (e.g., less than 500 pieces) and a custom offset-printing job wouldn't be economical.

Internet printers keep their prices low by combining multiple print jobs into one. This means your paper choices are limited. Also, every print job is done in *process color*, which involves four basic ink colors—cyan, magenta, yellow, black—being combined to simulate other colors. Most commercial full-color printing is done using process color. But for stationery, it's usually best to use *spot color*, where each color gets its own print run. Colors printed with process color will contain a noticeable dot pattern; colors printed with spot color will not. This dot pattern can also make small text printed in process colors look gritty. The only safe color is black.

The cheapest option is to make letterhead yourself with your laser printer. If you think that would be anathema to a typography snob like me, think again. In fact, I'm not ashamed to admit it—I only use laser-printed letterhead.

Why? My law practice consists of one lawyer who never mails a letter if an e-mail or PDF will suffice. I use so little letterhead that it's never been economical to have it professionally printed. I imagine

You don't need a graphic designer if you hire a letterpress printer. Letterpress printers are usually limited to the fonts they have on hand, so they're in the best position to handle the design work. But it is possible to convert digital files to plates that can be printed by letterpress.

THE LAW OFFICES OF

**CADMIUM Q.
EAGLEFEATHER**

PLC

5419 HOLLYWOOD BLVD STE C731
LOS ANGELES CA 90027
323 555 1435
323 555 1439 FAX

12985 BALDWIN DR STE B22
MAKAWAO HI 96768
808 555 5435
808 555 5439 FAX

CADMIUM@CQELAW.COM

January 15, 2010

George Falkenburg
Falkenburg, Fester, and Funk LLP
1252 W. 83rd Street
New York, NY 10012

Re: *Nicholson v. Amygdala Inc.,*
          Case No. B718590125-2

Dear Mr. Falkenburg:

In response to your recent request, enclosed is a DVD of photographs I took during the inspection of the Amygdala facility on October 30, 2009.

I apologize for the delay, but I was recently hospitalized for a concussion sustained while rollerblading. Rest assured that I am on the mend.

If you have any questions regarding this DVD, please let me know.

Sincerely,

CADMIUM Q. EAGLEFEATHER

CQE / bqe
Enclosure

Code 18901   This version has a more modern look, with a two-column layout and a simplified address block.

LETTERHEAD   189

that describes an increasing number of law offices. So for them, some tips.

Laser-printed letterhead often looks flat and cheap. Therefore, you must overcome the three telltale signs of laser-printed letterhead.

(1) *The typography is terrible.* That's been covered above—take the same care with your letterhead typography that you would if you were going to spend $5,000 printing it.

Dedicated paper stores like Kelly Paper (kellypaper.com) stock the best selection of laser-printable letterhead paper. Office-supply stores don't usually carry the good stuff.

(2) *It's printed on basic white printer paper.* Splurge on some deluxe paper at your local specialty-paper store. (I use Crane's Crest cotton paper. It's not cheap.) Get off-white or ivory paper—pure white tends to highlight flaws in the laser printing. Choose *wove* paper, which is smooth, rather than *laid* paper, which has a ribbed texture. Laser toner affixes better to a smooth surface. (More about this in PRINTERS AND PAPER.)

(3) *The name and address are printed in black.* Compared to black printing ink, black laser toner has a characteristic luster, and is usually closer to dark gray than black. Heighten the illusion by printing the name and address in a color—something pale and noncontroversial. Color laser printers also use process color, so run tests to make sure the color you pick doesn't have a gritty dot pattern. Grayish-blue tones often work well.

WORKING WITH A GRAPHIC DESIGNER

Graphic designers are everywhere, at every price point. As with offset printers, I wish I could say that price and quality correlate, but they don't.

This is an error clients make when selecting lawyers, too. If you don't like bossy clients, don't be one.

The most common error made by people hiring graphic designers is devoting too little time to selecting the designer, and too much time to critiquing the design work. Instead, spend all the time you want choosing a designer. But once you choose, get out of the way and let the designer do their thing. You'll get better results.

These days, any graphic designer worth their salt has an online portfolio. Reviewing online portfolios is the easiest way to find potential designers.

It's fine to ask a graphic designer to show you samples of work they've done for similar clients. It's also fine to ask for a detailed proposal with deliverables and budget. But I recommend getting detailed proposals from only two designers, and at most three—after that you'll be hopelessly confused.

<aside>If you're worried about paying for work you don't like, put approval milestones in the contract that give you the option to terminate for a pro rata fee.</aside>

It's not fine to ask a graphic designer to work for free, or for a discount, or on spec. If you don't like the fee, you can always find someone cheaper. Creative professionals often need more legal advice than they can afford, so barter may be an option.

Beyond the design advantages, a graphic designer will often know of good local printers and will work with the printer to get the job done—so you don't have to.

If you hire a graphic designer to make your letterhead, always test sample designs by printing out a real letter, or have the designer mock one up. You can't decide on letterhead just by looking at the name and address block in isolation. As these examples illustrate, everything has to work together.

<aside>Consensus kills. If you work at a big firm, approval authority for creative work should be vested in a small group of people—four at most, with a designated leader. You'll never please everyone, so there's no point in trying.</aside>

BY THE WAY

➤   Lawyers typically live up to their reputation of being risk-averse. So why do some big firms use letterhead that lists all their partners (and sometimes also their associates)? If a lawyer joins the firm, the letterhead has to be reprinted. If a lawyer leaves the firm, the letterhead has to be reprinted. While the firm awaits the new letterhead, the current letterhead lists a departed attorney, which is possibly an ethics violation. (See, e.g., ABA Model Rules of Prof. Conduct 7.5 and 7.1; Calif. Rule of Prof. Conduct 1-400(A)(2).) Furthermore, all those names waste a lot of space and usually have to be printed so small that they're barely legible. Bottom line: bad idea.

business cards

Shrink and simplify

Business cards, like CAPTION PAGES, have to fit a lot of information in a small area. But they often try to do too much.

For instance, the card layout below is fairly common among lawyers. I call it the baseball-diamond layout: information is pushed out to the corners, and your eye has to travel around the edge of the whole card to read everything.

BUSINESS LITIGATION
PERSONAL INJURY
MARITIME DISPUTES

ADMITTED IN CALIFORNIA AND HAWAII

THE LAW OFFICES OF

Cadmium Q. Eaglefeather

A PROFESSIONAL LAW CORPORATION

5419 HOLLYWOOD BLVD. STE. C731
LOS ANGELES, CALIFORNIA 90027

TEL: (323) 555-1435
FAX: (323) 555-1439
CADMIUM@CQELAW.COM

Code 19201

BEFORE

GOOFY FONT used for name.
Copperplate font used for other text.
POINT SIZE of name too large.
No LETTERSPACING in caps.
Information pushed out to corners.

The guiding principles with business cards are the same as with LETTERHEAD. Remove anything nonessential. Don't worry about the text being small—there's not very much of it. Build the layout from the text outward. The white space will take care of itself. If you work from the edges of the card inward, you're more likely to end up with a baseball diamond.

```
┌──────────────────────────────────────────────┐
│                                                │
│                                                │
│                                                │
│     The Law Offices of                         │
│   ∝  Cadmium Q. Eaglefeather, PLC              │
│                                                │
│                                                │
│     5419 Hollywood Blvd, Ste C731   Los Angeles CA 90027 │
│     323 555-1435   323 555-1439 FAX            │
│     cadmium@cqelaw.com                          │
│                                                │
│                                                │
└──────────────────────────────────────────────┘
```

Code 19301

AFTER

One non-goofy font used for all text.
Point size more reasonable and consistent.
Text layout simplified.
Pomposity eliminated.

PRODUCTION TIPS FOR BUSINESS CARDS

See the notes under LETTERHEAD for general tips about getting stationery items designed and printed.

In addition to those tips, carefully consider the paper stock for your business cards. More than other printed items, business cards provide a tactile experience, much like shaking someone's hand. A business card should feel great between your fingers. I've gotten too many cards from lawyers that felt like valet-parking receipts.

For that reason, I can't endorse laser-printed business cards. The sheets of perforated cards designed for laser printing are made of thin and cheap paper, and the resulting business cards are flimsy and sad. Get them professionally printed.

Color can be a nice touch on business cards, but it has to be understated. The louder the color, the less of it you can use, and vice versa.

résumés

Avoid dense text by using a second page

During law school, I interviewed for a job at a small law firm. One of the hiring partner's first comments was "It's so unusual that I see a résumé without any typos."

"Are you serious?" I said.

She said, "Yes, probably 90% of the résumés I get have typos. And that includes the ones we get from the top schools."

I got the job. Probably there were better-qualified candidates, but they damaged their chances with sloppy résumés. The irony is that those people, who most needed to hear this hiring partner's feedback, weren't in the room. Because they never got an interview.

This is a book on typography, not typos, but nothing beats having another person—or even better, more than one—edit your résumé. Insist that each reviewer propose at least three edits.

Consider yourself warned.

The biggest problem I see with résumés is that they are uncomfortably dense with text. I take this to be the influence of the myth that a résumé can only be one page long.

Résumé is the original spelling and still preferred. **Resumé** is acceptable. **Resume** is common but wrong. See the table on the inside back cover to learn how to type the é character.

Unless a potential employer demands one page, feel free to make your résumé two pages. Or longer, if necessary. This will ease your typographic problems. Two caveats, however. Don't assume a reader will get past the first page—put the most important information up front. And when I say "if necessary," remember you're writing for a potential employer, not your mom. My résumé fits on two pages. I'll bet yours can too.

Print a two-page résumé with two sheets of paper, even if you have a duplex printer. You don't want a potential employer to overlook the second page because it's printed on the back of the first.

BEFORE

1. PAGE MARGINS too small; LINE LENGTH too big.
   All text set in Calibri (a SYSTEM FONT).

2. Headings and gray boxes are too large relative to body text.
   Key information—the where and when—is buried.
   Ugly BULLETED LISTS.

3. Too much information on one page.

TRIXIE B. ARGON

5419 HOLLYWOOD BLVD. STE. C731, LOS ANGELES CA 90027   (323) 555-1435   TRIXIEARGON @GMAIL.COM

Education

UCLA School of Law   Los Angeles, California
August 2007 to June 2010
❖ Cumulative GPA: 3.98
❖ Academic interests: real-estate financing, criminal procedure, corporations
❖ California Bar Exam results pending

Harvard University   Cambridge, Massachusetts
September 2002 to June 2006
❖ B.A. summa cum laude, Economics
❖ Extensive coursework in Astrophysics, Statistics
❖ Van Damme Scholarship

Legal experience

Falkenburg, Fester & Funk LLP   New York, New York
November 2008 to present
Law clerk
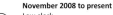
❖ Handled various litigation matters in state and federal court, including:
❖ An unlawful detainer action
❖ A demurrer to a breach-of-contract lawsuit in state court
❖ Oppositions to motions to dismiss in federal court (Fed. R. Civ. P. 12(b), 12(e), 9(b))
❖ Development of evidence for Internet trademark and copyright infringement actions, including statistical analysis

Other work experience

Proximate Cause   Los Angeles, California
June 2006 to May 2007
Assistant to the Director
❖ Helped devise fundraising campaigns for this innovative nonprofit
❖ Handled lunch orders and general errands

Hot Topic   Boston, Massachusetts
February 2003 to March 2005
Retail sales associate
❖ Top in-store sales associate in seven out of eight quarters
❖ Inventory management
❖ Training and recruiting

Skills and interests

❖ Fluent in Mandarin, Esperanto; conversational knowledge of Gaelic
❖ Writer of U.S. Senate-themed fan fiction
❖ Ocean kayaking and free diving
❖ Travel, cooking, hiking, playing with my dog
❖ Ceramics

Code 19501

AFTER

- (1) Page margins bigger; line length smaller. No more Calibri.

- (2) Headings are smaller and lighter. Names of schools and businesses are larger. Gentler list bullets.

- (3) Nonessential information moved to second page.

Keep in mind that one way a résumé illustrates your virtues is by drawing connections between you—whom the reader knows nothing about—and various schools and employers, which the reader may have heard of. The implied syllogism goes like this: *Falkenburg, Fester & Funk is an elite firm; this person worked at Falkenburg; therefore, this person is an elite-quality lawyer.* Don't make your reader struggle to dig out the names of those schools and employers—make sure they're immediately visible.

In this revision, the visual emphasis has shifted from the headings—who cares about résumé headings?—to the substance. This also makes the résumé more skimmable, which is never a bad thing.

PRODUCTION TIPS FOR RÉSUMÉS

I treat a résumé as a special kind of laser-printed LETTERHEAD. Review the production tips on page 190.

Past that, resist the urge to buy paper specially marketed for résumés—the kinds that come in odd colors (e.g., green, pink, gray) or textures (e.g., parchment, marble, linen). High-quality business-letterhead paper from the stationery store is just fine. Anything more elaborate looks overbaked.

Increasingly, employers and recruiters are asking for résumés in PDF format. In PDF, good typography survives; good paper is irrelevant.

TRIXIE B. ARGON

5419 HOLLYWOOD BLVD. STE. C731, LOS ANGELES CA 90027

(323) 555-1435   TRIXIEARGON @ GMAIL.COM

Education

UCLA School of Law   2007–10

▫ Cumulative GPA: 3.98
▫ Academic interests: real-estate financing, criminal procedure, corporations
▫ California Bar Exam results pending

Harvard University   2002–06

▫ B.A. *summa cum laude*, Economics
▫ Extensive coursework in Astrophysics, Statistics
▫ Van Damme Scholarship

Legal experience

Falkenburg, Fester & Funk LLP   2008–now

Law clerk

▫ Handled various litigation matters in state and federal court, including:
▫ An unlawful detainer action
▫ A demurrer to a breach-of-contract lawsuit in state court
▫ Oppositions to motions to dismiss in federal court (Fed. R. Civ. P. 12(b), 12(e), 9(b))
▫ Development of evidence for Internet trademark and copyright infringement actions, including statistical analysis

Other work experience

Proximate Cause   2006–07

Assistant to the Director

▫ Helped devise fundraising campaigns for this innovative nonprofit
▫ Handled lunch orders and general errands

Hot Topic   2003–05

Retail sales associate

▫ Top in-store sales associate in seven out of eight quarters
▫ Inventory management
▫ Training and recruiting

ARGON RÉSUMÉ — PAGE 1 OF 2

Code 19701

For more tips and tools, visit the Typography for Lawyers website at

typographyforlawyers.com

Appendix

How to interpret court rules

Among legal documents, court filings must conform to the narrowest typographic restrictions—court rules. But except for a few jurisdictions, court rules still give lawyers a fair amount of typographic latitude.

So why do 99.99% of the court filings in any jurisdiction look alike?

One reason is the bandwagon effect. Lawyers usually assume that all the other lawyers are following the rules, so if everyone uses 12-point TIMES NEW ROMAN, or puts two vertical lines in the left margin, it must be that the court demands it. Possible, but unlikely. Read your court rules carefully—you'll probably be surprised at how much is left to your discretion.

Another reason is fear. "The judge will sanction me because my filings aren't as ugly and hard to read as everyone else's." Again—possible, but unlikely. If your typography conforms to the court rules in good faith, you should be on solid ground. I've never had a judge complain about the unusually good typography in my filings.

A third reason is force of habit. To create today's filing, lawyers will often just start with last week's filing, which was based on the filing from the week before that, and so on. Formatting choices get entrenched even if they don't relate to the rules.

A fourth reason is lack of typographic skill. How do you depart from the usual dreck while still adhering to the rules? Armed with the information in this book, you should have no problem understanding where court rules are strict and where they're flexible.

WHY HAVE COURT RULES ABOUT TYPOGRAPHY?

Consistency of typography in court filings helps ensure fairness to the parties. For instance, in jurisdictions that use page limits, if lawyer A sets all his briefs at 12 point, and lawyer B sets all hers at 10 point, lawyer B gets the advantage of more words per page. Court rules about typography prevent abuse of these limits.

Court rules about typography also exist as a convenience to the judge and the court staff. Judges don't want to read sheaves of nine-point text. Rules that set minimum PAGE MARGINS or POINT SIZE ensure a minimum standard of legibility.

As you put your typographic discretion to work, keep these two goals in mind. Don't expect your judge to be happy if you exploit typographic loopholes in the rules that defeat these goals.

For instance, the U.S. District Court for the Central District of California allows court filings to be set in a proportionally spaced font that's 14 point or larger. (C.D. Cal. L.R. 11-3.1.1.) How about this one? It's proportionally spaced. It's set at 14 point. It's also very condensed so I can fit a lot more words on the page. Technically speaking, I've complied with the rule. But will a federal judge be impressed with how I've interpreted the rule? No way.

Conversely, you shouldn't worry about typographic improvements that result in *fewer* words per page, like larger page margins. Unless you need every word or every page allocated to you—and good legal writers never do—why not use the extra white space to improve the typography? (See MOTIONS for an example.)

Be careful—court rules about typography are not designed to produce good typography. That's your job. Court rules set minimums and maximums. They are usually phrased in terms of "at least" and "no more than." Very rarely do they completely eliminate discretion.

I'm not suggesting you should use this discretion to be different for the sake of being different. Rather, you should use this discretion to fill in what the court rules deliberately leave incomplete. Otherwise, your typography will be arbitrary—the result of the rules being summed together without judgment or nuance.

I'm aware that some judges have house rules that may be unwritten, or that may conflict with rules of the jurisdiction, but that lawyers in front of these judges ignore at their peril. Typography is about being effective. If the only font your judge wants to see is Arial Bold Condensed, then that's the way it is.

TEXT FORMATTING

If the rule calls for a monospaced font sized in "characters per inch," divide 120 by this measure to get the equivalent point size. Likewise, divide 120 by point size to get characters per inch.

(1) If the rules call for a specific font or point size, use it. For instance, Florida Rule of Appellate Procedure 9.210(a)(2) requires either 14-point Times New Roman or 12-point Courier New. In that case, you have no discretion. Follow the rule.

(2) If the rules offer a choice between a MONOSPACED FONT and anything else, choose the latter.

(3) If the rules call for a font that's similar to a particular font, use your discretion carefully. For instance, Calif. Rule of Court 2.105 requires a font "essentially equivalent to Courier, Times New Roman, or Arial." I take this to mean you should use a font that has the general legibility and length characteristics of Courier, Times New Roman, or Arial. (In other words,

pretty much any font in FONT SAMPLES.) I don't take the rule to mean you can use only those three fonts. If the rule meant that, it would've said so.

(4) If the rules allow you to use either a serif or a sans serif font (see page 85) for BODY TEXT, I strongly recommend a serif font. Most books, newspapers, and magazines use serif fonts for body text. It's the traditional choice and still the best choice.

(5) If the rules call for a proportionally spaced font, use your discretion. Just about every font is proportionally spaced, so this kind of rule doesn't create a meaningful limitation. A tasteful serif font, like the ones in FONT SAMPLES, is the best bet.

(6) If the rules set a minimum point size, use the minimum. For instance, many courts require that text be set at 12 point or larger. As you know from POINT SIZE, 12 point is already pretty big. No need to go bigger. (I've only found a handful of courts that permit 11 point, and none that permit 10 point.)

PAGE LAYOUT

(1) The rules may allow PAGE MARGINS that result in oversize LINE LENGTHS. Feel free to widen the page margins to get a more reasonable line length. For instance, Calif. Rule of Court 2.107 requires margins "at least one inch from the left edge ... [and] at least 1/2 inch from the right edge." At maximum, this creates seven-inch lines, which will be too long for most 12-point fonts. The "at least" qualifier in the rule is a signal that you need not fill up every square inch.

(2) Likewise, the rules may allow you to fit a certain number of lines per page. You may want to use fewer if it makes for a more legible and appealing layout. Remember the ninth MAXIM OF PAGE LAYOUT—*don't fear white space*.

③ LINE SPACING rules should be interpreted arithmetically, not as word-processor lingo. If a rule calls for double-spaced lines, set your line spacing to exactly twice the point size of the body text. Don't rely on the "Double" line spacing option in your word processor, which may not be equivalent. For instance, in Word, "Double" line spacing is about 15% larger than true double spacing. This reduces the number of lines per page.

④ Avoid putting RULES AND BORDERS within or around the page that aren't explicitly required. It clutters the page and constricts the text. For example, in the state and federal courts in Los Angeles, almost every litigator puts two vertical lines on the left edge of the page, and one vertical line on the right. But this practice is not required by any rule. In California state court, the line on the left is optional—you can use a solid single or double line, but you can also use a "vertical column of space at least 1/5 inch wide." (Calif. Rule of Court 2.108(4).) Nothing is required on the right side. Meanwhile, our federal court requires no vertical lines on either side. Follow the rules—not the crowd.

⑤ If the court rules explicitly require vertical lines, make them no more than half a point thick. This will keep them relatively unobtrusive.

NOTE FOR ELECTRONIC FILERS

The tips above apply equally to PDFs. PDFs preserve your formatting exactly, including fonts, so you don't have to worry that readers will see something different from what you intended.

But if you have to file certain documents (e.g., proposed orders) as Word or WordPerfect files, be careful. Word-processor file formats require the recipient to have the same fonts installed. Therefore, to be safe, set these documents in TIMES NEW ROMAN or another standard SYSTEM FONT to ensure they display accurately.

Printers and paper

As I mentioned in the introduction, it really doesn't matter what word-processing program you use—all of them are capable of producing good typography.

But your printer and paper can make a big difference in the final result. As your eye for typography gets better, you'll start to notice that not all printers are alike.

(I am not a compensated endorser of any products mentioned below. These recommendations reflect my experiences. Yours may vary.)

INKJET PRINTER OR LASER PRINTER?

Laser. Inkjet printers used to be the cheaper and lower-quality alternative to laser printers. Inkjets are a lot better than they were 20 years ago, but they still can't equal the crisp edges of laser printing.

Why? Inkjet printers work by spraying small droplets of liquid ink onto the paper, which start out wet and then dry in the air. The wet droplets spread slightly as they're absorbed into the paper. That's a desirable effect for photographs, because it helps blend adjacent colors, and it's why inkjets are preferred for photo printing. It's not desirable for text, because it makes edges less distinct. And as the text gets smaller, the problem becomes more pronounced.

Laser printers work by depositing particles of dry toner onto the paper and then fusing the toner to the paper with heat. This creates a sharper edge on the printed page and makes laser printers better suited for printing text.

Over the years, laser printers have also gotten a lot cheaper. So there's no reason for a law office to use an inkjet printer.

POSTSCRIPT OR NOT?

Before a printer can render a page, the layout on the screen has to be converted into an intermediate format using a *page-description language*. If you ever wondered what a printer driver does, that's what.

The **PDF** file format is built on a subset of the PostScript language. PDF was a proprietary Adobe format until 2008, when it became an open standard.

PostScript is a proprietary page-description language owned by Adobe. In the '80s, most laser printers were built on PostScript, in much the same way that most computers today are built on Windows. As laser-printing hardware became cheaper to manufacture, printer makers sought alternatives to PostScript with lower licensing fees.

Most printers today don't use licensed PostScript. The main alternative is PostScript *emulation*, which approximates PostScript using non-Adobe technology. Other page-description languages exist—the most common one is *PCL*, owned by Hewlett-Packard and found mostly in their printers.

Why should you care?

First, different page-description languages—and different emulations of a page-description language—will render a given document slightly differently. In my experience, those differences are often most noticeable in the quality of printed text, and that quality can vary widely.

Second, no printer can ever be better than its printer driver. Garbage in, garbage out. Even if a printer has excellent technical specifications—great resolution and print speed—it can be hobbled by a bad driver. And if it turns out your printer has bad driver software, there's not much you can do except buy a different printer.

Among page-description languages, PostScript is still the gold standard. It dominates professional publishing. Therefore, if you want the best printed output, consider a printer that uses true licensed PostScript. (For instance, most members of the Xerox Phaser line of printers. I own one of these.)

If you're considering a printer that uses PostScript emulation, scrutinize its output before you buy. Get samples of black text at various sizes. Ignore the ritzy color photo that most printers use as their automatic test page. That photo may be pretty, but it won't tell you anything about how the printer performs with text-heavy documents.

PHOTOCOPY OR PRINT?

A photocopier used to be an indispensable tool in a law office. But a photocopier is just a laser printer with a camera attached. As laser printers have gotten faster, the photocopier has become less essential.

For text documents, copies made direct from the laser printer will always look better than photocopies. The cost per page will also be somewhat higher.

For image-intensive documents—for instance, scanned discovery—the photocopier will always be faster.

Online printer reviewers claim to evaluate text quality, but their standards are lax, and their judgments subjective.

Printer resolution (usually rated in **DPI**, or **dots per inch**) can be a misleading metric. Printer hardware can only output a fixed number of dots in a square inch (for instance, 600 × 600). But printer makers will often claim "effective" resolutions of 2400 × 600 or more, usually the result of puffery and dubious math. Caveat emptor.

COLOR OR MONOCHROME?

If I could have only one laser printer, it would be a color laser printer. But I have two—one color, one monochrome—so I know that the monochrome performance of a color laser printer is not as good as a dedicated monochrome printer in the same price range. This makes sense—a color laser printer is really four laser printers sharing a single paper path.

If you truly never print color, there's no need for a color laser printer.

Though I have dissuaded you from using COLOR for text in documents, it's fine to use color images as illustrations or exhibits.

Beware—makers of color laser printers soft-pedal the costs of color output, usually with optimistic assumptions about how many pages a color toner cartridge will produce. Always check the cost of replacement toner cartridges before buying a color printer, and remember that every sheet of color output depletes four cartridges simultaneously.

Also beware of entry-level color laser printers. While fine for occasional use, they are easily overwhelmed by large image files (for instance, PDFs of scanned discovery). Lawyers who rely on cheap color printers usually find this out at an inopportune moment, like 20 minutes before a filing deadline.

DUPLEX OR SIMPLEX?

A *duplex* printer can print on both sides of a sheet of paper; a *simplex* printer only prints on one side.

Litigators who serve a lot of documents by mail will also enjoy the cheaper postage for duplex-printed documents.

If you care at all about the environmental impact that lawyering has on the world, get a duplex printer. A duplexing unit is often available as an accessory for simplex printers. You don't have to print fewer pages. You'll just be printing them on half the number of sheets of paper. What's not to like?

I shed a tear whenever a lawyer sends me a document that's not printed duplex. That means I wipe a lot of tears. Folks, we have the technology. Let's use it.

One caveat: if you switch to duplex printing, you may need to get paper that's more opaque, so the printing on one side doesn't show through to the other.

PAPER

As noted above, laser printers work by depositing dry toner onto paper and fusing it onto the paper using heated metal rollers. A piece of paper has a naturally uneven surface. The more uneven the surface, the less well the toner adheres to the paper when it goes through the rollers. (Think about sticking a stamp on an envelope vs. sticking it on a brick.)

For best results, use the smoothest paper you can find. Choose paper designated "laser" over paper designated "copy" or "inkjet"—these varieties tend to be less smooth. I use Hammermill Laser Print because it's smooth, opaque, and very bright. (Among papers, *brightness* measures how well the paper reflects white light.)

If you go shopping for nicer paper at the stationery store (e.g., to use as LETTERHEAD), choose *wove* paper, which is smooth, rather than *laid* paper, which has a ribbed texture. Toner affixes better to wove paper.

How to make a PDF

There's a right way and a wrong way to make a PDF. Based on an unscientific survey of the PDFs I get from other lawyers, just about all of you are doing it the wrong way.

The wrong way: print the document on paper and scan it to PDF.

The right way: "print" the document directly to PDF.

HOW TO PRINT DIRECTLY TO PDF

WINDOWS | *Install a printer driver that outputs PDFs instead of sending a file to a physical printer. If you have a commercial version of Adobe Acrobat (not just the free Acrobat Reader), the ‹Adobe PDF› driver should already be installed. If you don't have Adobe Acrobat, numerous third-party PDF printer drivers are available. When you issue the print command, you'll see the ‹Print› dialog box. At the top of this box is a popup menu listing the installed printers. Select your PDF printer. Set other options as needed and click ‹OK›.*

MAC | *You don't need a special print driver—printing directly to PDF is built into the Mac operating system. Issue the print command. The dialog box that appears has a button at the lower left labeled ‹PDF›. Click this button. From the menu that appears, select ‹Save as PDF›. In the next dialog box, enter a filename and click ‹Save›.*

"What's the difference? Either way, you end up with a PDF." True. But one PDF is much better than the other.

When you print a document and then scan it to PDF, you're defeating most of the benefits of using a PDF at all. Essentially, you're making a series of photos of your document and packaging them inside a PDF. These photos occupy a lot of disk space, they're slow to view or print, they have to go through OCR to be searchable, and any care you've put into typography will be diluted by the reduced quality of the scan.

But printing directly to PDF stores your document in a compact, high-resolution format. Instead of a series of photos, the document pages are stored as a series of scalable mathematical shapes (or *vector graphics* as they're sometimes known). These shapes take up very little space on disk, are fast to view or print, are searchable without OCR, and preserve your typography with perfect fidelity. (If you have bitmap images in your document, like JPEGs, they will still be stored in the PDF as bitmaps.)

What about fonts? When you print directly to PDF, fonts are embedded in the PDF as necessary to preserve the text formatting. So readers of the document will always see your intended fonts, even if they don't have the same fonts installed on their machines.

"But my document has exhibits. How am I supposed to get those into the word-processing document?" You don't. Print the word-processing document to PDF as described above. Then add the exhibits to the PDF using Acrobat or another PDF-editing tool.

Got it? Good.

Bibliography

This is not, by any measure, a comprehensive bibliography. Rather, it's a selection of favorites from my own bookshelf that I consult most frequently in my work as a lawyer and a typographer.

LEGAL WRITING

Bryan A. Garner, *Garner's Modern American Usage*, 3rd ed. (New York: Oxford University Press, 2009).

———, *Garner's Dictionary of Legal Usage*, 3rd ed. (New York: Oxford University Press, 2011).

———, *The Redbook: A Manual on Legal Style*, 2nd ed. (Eagan, Minnesota: Thomson West, 2006).

———, *The Winning Brief*, 2nd ed. (New York: Oxford University Press, 2004).

Antonin Scalia and Bryan A. Garner, *Making Your Case: The Art of Persuading Judges* (Eagan, Minnesota: Thomson West, 2008).

Long before he agreed to write the foreword for this book, Bryan Garner was a hero of mine. Garner thinks and writes about American English in a way that's rigorous, convincing, and accessible. He is stern but not shrill; authoritative but not authoritarian. He is a vigorous advocate for clear, simple writing—especially legal writing. His work should be mandatory reading for all lawyers.

TYPOGRAPHY

Jan Middendorp, *Shaping Text* (Amsterdam: BIS Publishers, 2012).

> If you get a second book on typography, get this one. Middendorp's beautifully written and illustrated book is full of careful details and lucid explanations.

Robert Bringhurst, *The Elements of Typographic Style*, 4th ed. (Vancouver: Hartley and Marks Publishers, 2013).

> Bringhurst's book is a standard reference guide among professional typographers, bringing together the history, theory, and practice of typography.

Ellen Lupton, *Thinking With Type*, 2nd ed. (New York: Princeton Architectural Press, 2010).

> Intended as an introduction to typography for design students, Lupton's book is more accessible than Bringhurst's. It includes color illustrations from every era of typography.

Erik Spiekermann and E. M. Ginger, *Stop Stealing Sheep & Find Out How Type Works*, 2nd ed. (Berkeley, California: Adobe Press, 2002).

> Focuses on fonts—how they differ in appearance and in function. (My font Hermes is among those featured.)

DESIGN PRINCIPLES

Edward Tufte, *The Visual Display of Quantitative Information*, 2nd ed. (Cheshire, Connecticut: Graphics Press, 2001).

———, *Envisioning Information*, 4th printing ed. (Cheshire, Connecticut: Graphics Press, 1990).

> These are two of my favorite books. Tufte makes an eloquent and compelling case for why design matters. Both books are fantastically interesting, featuring examples of information design from many historical periods.

William Lidwell, Kritina Holden, and Jill Butler, *Universal Principles of Design*, 2nd ed. (Beverly, Massachusetts: Rockport Publishers, 2010).

> An excellent and accessible introduction to design principles that apply not only to printed documents, but to all objects that we interact with.

OTHER WORKS CITED

The Chicago Manual of Style, 16th ed. (Chicago: University of Chicago Press, 2010).

United States Court of Appeals for the Seventh Circuit, *Requirements and Suggestions for Typography in Briefs and Other Papers*, available at http://www.ca7.uscourts.gov/Rules/type.pdf

Edward W. Jessen, *California Style Manual*, 4th ed. (San Francisco: West Group, 2000).

The Bluebook: A Uniform System of Citation, 19th ed. (Cambridge, Massachusetts: The Harvard Law Review Association, 2010).

Acknowledgments

Thank you to everyone who has visited the Typography for Lawyers website or passed it along to friends. Thank you especially to those who have written me with compliments, corrections, or suggestions.

Thank you to Jason Wilson and Baird Craft at Jones McClure Publishing (jonesmcclure.com) for approaching me about doing this book.

Thank you to Jonathan Kirsch (jonathankirsch.com) for legal assistance.

Thank you to the typographers and lawyers who have been generous to me over the years with their time and expertise: Gino Lee, David Berlow (fontbureau.com), Matthew Carter (carterand cone.com), Robert Powsner, Bill Rubenstein (billrubenstein.com), Lynne Coffin, and Alan Schlosser. Most of what I know about these topics can be traced to one of these people.

Thank you to William Lidwell and Jill Butler, authors of *Universal Principles of Design*, for permission to reprint their butterfly-ballot diagrams.

For providing fonts for the font-sample section, my thanks to Mark van Bronkhorst at MVB Fonts (mvbfonts.com), Jackson Cavanaugh at Okay Type Foundry (okaytype.com), Allan Haley at Monotype Imaging (monotypeimaging.com), Michael Hochleitner at Typejockeys (typejockeys.com), Jonathan Hoefler at Hoefler & Frere-Jones (typography.com), Zuzana Licko at Emigre (emigre.com), Eric Olson at Process Type Foundry (processtypefoundry.com), Harry Parker at the Font Bureau (fontbureau.com), Christian Schwartz at Commercial Type (commercialtype.com), Kris Sowersby at Klim Type Foundry (klim.co.nz), Erik Spiekermann at FSI FontShop International (fontshop.com), Sumner Stone at Stone Type Foundry (stonetypefoundry.com), František Štorm at Storm Type Foundry (stormtype.com), and Sue Zafarana at Bitstream (bitstream.com).

Thank you to those who read and commented on drafts of the book: Patrick Anderson, Jessica Coffin Butterick, Don Cruse, Briana Hill, Andrew Kaplan, Derek Kiernan-Johnson, Indra Kupferschmid, Russ Mitchell, Alfredo Paloyo, Michael Rescorla, Kent Richland, and Sara Richland.

Thank you to Allan Haley and Mike Parker for sharing their expertise about the history of Times New Roman.

Thank you to Bryan Garner for writing the foreword.

Thank you to Jack Arthur, Jenny Sulak, Kathryn Hunter, Kathryn Ritcheske, and the rest of the team at Jones McClure Publishing for helping get the book into the hands of readers.

I welcome suggestions for future revisions of the book. You can reach me at mb@typographyforlawyers.com.

IMAGE CREDITS

COLOPHON

Body text was set in **Lyon Text**, designed by Kai Bernau. Lyon is based on of 16th-century French typography. Available from Commercial Type (commercialtype.com).

Sidebars, technical instructions, and captions were set in **Concourse**, designed by Matthew Butterick. Concourse is inspired by geometric sans serifs of the 1930s. Available from MB Type (concoursefont.com).

Topic headlines were set in **Cheltenham FB**, designed by David Berlow. Monospaced text was set in **FB Alix**, designed by Matthew Butterick. Both are available from the Font Bureau (fontbureau.com).

Chapter headings were set in the display version of **Harriet**, designed by Jackson Cavanaugh. Available from Okay Type Foundry (harrietseries.com).

List indexes (①②③) were set in **Whitney Index**, available from Hoefler & Frere-Jones (typography.com).

The text on the front cover is **FF Quadraat Sans**, designed by Fred Smeijers. Available from FSI FontShop International (fontshop.com).

Except for Cheltenham FB and Whitney Index, all these fonts appear in FONT SAMPLES with web codes for more information.

Book designed by Matthew Butterick with Adobe InDesign.

MATTHEW BUTTERICK got his B.A. degree *magna cum laude* from Harvard University in visual & environmental studies. Butterick's typographic work is in the permanent collection of the Houghton Library at Harvard.

Butterick started his career as a font designer and engineer, working for David Berlow and Matthew Carter on fonts for Apple, Microsoft, Ziff Davis, and others. His work was featured in FUSE, Neville Brody's journal of experimental typography. Butterick designed the fonts Herald Gothic, Wessex, and the popular sans serif family Hermes.

At the beginning of the Internet era, Butterick moved to San Francisco and founded Atomic Vision, a website design and engineering company. Butterick and his staff created websites for Internet pioneers like CNET, Netscape, VeriSign, and *Wired* magazine.

Atomic Vision was acquired by open-source software developer Red Hat. Butterick was part of the management team behind Red Hat's successful IPO.

Butterick attended UCLA law school and became a member of the California bar in 2007. He has released three fonts tailored to the needs of legal writers: FB Alix, Concourse, and Equity. In 2012, for his work in legal typography, he received the Legal Writing Institute's Golden Pen Award.

Butterick is also an accomplished pianist and musician whose credits include the San Francisco production of *Hedwig and the Angry Inch*.

Butterick lives in the Hollywood Hills with his wife Jessica and their boxer, Roxy.

BRYAN A. GARNER, president of LawProse, Inc., is the award-winning author of many books on legal writing and advocacy. He is the editor in chief of all editions of *Black's Law Dictionary*.

ACCENTED CHARACTERS

	WINDOWS	MAC	HTML		WINDOWS	MAC	HTML
á	alt 0225	option+e, a	&aacute;	î	alt 0238	option+i, i	&icirc;
Á	alt 0193	option+e, A	&Aacute;	Î	alt 0206	option+i, I	&Icirc;
à	alt 0224	option+ `, a	&agrave;	ï	alt 0239	option+u, i	&iuml;
À	alt 0192	option+ `, A	&Agrave;	Ï	alt 0207	option+u, I	&Iuml;
â	alt 0226	option+i, a	&acirc;	ñ	alt 0241	option+n, n	&ntilde;
Â	alt 0194	option+i, A	&Acirc;	Ñ	alt 0209	option+n, N	&Ntilde;
ä	alt 0228	option+u, a	&auml;	ó	alt 0243	option+e, o	&oacute;
Ä	alt 0196	option+u, A	&Auml;	Ó	alt 0211	option+e, O	&Oacute;
ã	alt 0227	option+n, a	&atilde;	ò	alt 0242	option+ `, o	&ograve;
Ã	alt 0195	option+n, A	&Atilde;	Ò	alt 0210	option+ `, O	&Ograve;
å	alt 0229	option+a	&aring;	ô	alt 0244	option+i, o	&ocirc;
Å	alt 0197	option+shift+a	&Aring;	Ô	alt 0212	option+i, O	&Ocirc;
æ	alt 0230	option+'	&aelig;	ö	alt 0246	option+u, o	&ouml;
Æ	alt 0198	option+shift+'	&AElig;	Ö	alt 0214	option+u, O	&Ouml;
ç	alt 0231	option+c	&ccedil;	õ	alt 0245	option+n, o	&otilde;
Ç	alt 0199	option+shift+c	&Ccedil;	Õ	alt 0213	option+n, O	&Otilde;
é	alt 0233	option+e, e	&eacute;	ø	alt 0248	option+o	&oslash;
É	alt 0201	option+e, E	&Eacute;	Ø	alt 0216	option+shift+o	&Oslash;
è	alt 0232	option+ `, e	&egrave;	œ	alt 0156	option+q	&oelig;
È	alt 0200	option+ `, E	&Egrave;	Œ	alt 0140	option+shift+q	&OElig;
ê	alt 0234	option+i, e	&ecirc;	ú	alt 0250	option+e, u	&uacute;
Ê	alt 0202	option+i, E	&Ecirc;	Ú	alt 0218	option+e, U	&Uacute;
ë	alt 0235	option+u, e	&euml;	ù	alt 0249	option+ `, u	&ugrave;
Ë	alt 0203	option+u, E	&Euml;	Ù	alt 0217	option+ `, U	&Ugrave;
í	alt 0237	option+e, i	&iacute;	û	alt 0251	option+i, u	&ucirc;
Í	alt 0205	option+e, I	&Iacute;	Û	alt 0219	option+i, U	&Ucirc;
ì	alt 0236	option+ `, i	&igrave;	ü	alt 0252	option+u, u	&uuml;
Ì	alt 0204	option+ `, I	&Igrave;	Ü	alt 0220	option+u, U	&Uuml;

WINDOWS | *With num lock active, hold down ‹alt› and type the four-digit code on the numeric keypad.*
MAC | *Type the two keys in sequence. Sequences are case-sensitive. ‹ ` › is the grave accent, at the left of the 1 key.*